W9-BZA-107

SPECTRUM
Test Prep

Grade 3

Spectrum

An imprint of Carson-Dellosa Publishing LLC
Greensboro, North Carolina

Spectrum
An imprint of Carson-Dellosa Publishing LLC
P.O. Box 35665
Greensboro, NC 27425 USA

Printed in the USA • All rights reserved.   ISBN 0-7696-8623-0

6 7 8 9 10 11 12 GLO 15 14 13 12 11 10

Table of Contents

Social Studies

Science

What's Inside?

This workbook is designed to help you and your third grader understand what he or she will be expected to know on standardized tests.

Practice Pages

The workbook is divided into four sections: English Language Arts, Mathematics, Social Studies, and Science. The practice activities in this workbook provide students with practice in each of these areas. Each section has practice activities that have questions similar to those that will appear on the standardized tests. Students should use a pencil to fill in the correct answers and to complete any writing on these activities.

National Standards

Before each practice section is a list of the national standards covered by that section. These standards list the knowledge and skills that students are expected to master at each grade level. The shaded *What it means* sections will help to explain any information in the standards that might be unfamiliar.

Mini-Tests and Final Tests

When your student finishes the practice pages for specific standards, your student can move on to a mini-test that covers the material presented on those practice activities. After an entire set of standards and accompanying practice pages are completed, your student should take the final tests, which incorporate materials from all the practice pages in that section.

Final Test Answer Sheet

The final tests have a separate answer sheet that mimics the style of the answer sheets the students will use on the standardized tests. The answer sheets appear at the end of each final test.

How Am I Doing?

The *How Am I Doing?* pages are designed to help students identify areas where they are proficient and areas where they still need more practice. They will pinpoint areas where more work is needed as well as areas where your student excels. Students can keep track of each of their mini-test scores on these pages.

Answer Key

Answers to all the practice pages, mini-tests, and final tests are listed by page number and appear at the end of the book.

To find a complete listing of the national standards in each subject area, you can access the following Web sites:

The National Council of Teachers of English: www.ncte.org
National Council of Teachers of Mathematics: www.nctm.org/standards
National Council for the Social Studies: www.ncss.org/standards
National Science Teachers Association: www.nsta.org/standards

English Language Arts Standards

Standard 1 *(See pages 9–11.)*
Students read a wide range of print and nonprint texts to build an understanding of texts, of themselves, and of the cultures of the United States and the world; to acquire new information; to respond to the needs and demands of society and the workplace; and for personal fulfillment. Among these texts are fiction and nonfiction, classic and contemporary works.

Standard 2 *(See pages 12–14.)*
Students read a wide range of literature from many periods in many genres to build an understanding of the many dimensions (e.g., philosophical, ethical, aesthetic) of human experience.

What it means:
- **Genre** is the type or category of literature. Some examples of genres include fiction, nonfiction, biographies, poetry, and fables. Each genre is categorized by various differences in form. For example, nonfiction differs from fiction in that it presents facts or tells a true story. The fable differs from the broader category of fiction because it has a moral or character lesson.

Standard 3 *(See pages 15–17.)*
Students apply a wide range of strategies to comprehend, interpret, evaluate, and appreciate texts. They draw on their prior experience, their interactions with other readers and writers, their knowledge of word meaning and of other texts, their word identification strategies, and their understanding of textual features (e.g., sound-letter correspondence, sentence structure, context, graphics).

What it means:
- Students should be able to use several different strategies to help them determine the meaning of unfamiliar words.

Standard 4 *(See pages 19–21.)*
Students adjust their use of spoken, written, and visual language (e.g., conventions, style, vocabulary) to communicate effectively with a variety of audiences and for different purposes.

Standard 5 *(See pages 22–25.)*
Students employ a wide range of strategies as they write and use different writing process elements appropriately to communicate with different audiences for a variety of purposes.

Standard 6 *(See pages 25–28.)*
Students apply knowledge of language structure, language conventions (e.g., spelling and punctuation), media techniques, figurative language, and genre to create, critique, and discuss print and nonprint texts.

What it means:
- **Figurative language** is language used for descriptive effect. It describes or implies meaning, rather than stating it directly. Similes, metaphors, hyperboles, and personification are types of figurative language.

English Language Arts Standards

Standard 7 *(See page 30.)*
Students conduct research on issues and interests by generating ideas and questions, and by posing problems. They gather, evaluate, and synthesize data from a variety of sources (e.g., print and nonprint texts, artifacts, people) to communicate their discoveries in ways that suit their purpose and audience.

Standard 8 *(See pages 31–32.)*
Students use a variety of technological and informational resources (e.g., libraries, databases, computer networks, video) to gather and synthesize information and to create and communicate knowledge.

Standard 9 *(See page 34.)*
Students develop an understanding of and respect for diversity in language use, patterns, and dialects across cultures, ethnic groups, geographic regions, and social roles.

Standard 10
Students whose first language is not English make use of their first language to develop competency in the English language arts and to develop understanding of content across the curriculum.

Standard 11 *(See page 35.)*
Students participate as knowledgeable, reflective, creative, and critical members of a variety of literacy communities.

Standard 12 *(See page 36.)*
Students use spoken, written, and visual language to accomplish their own purposes (e.g., for learning, enjoyment, persuasion, and the exchange of information).

English Language Arts

| 1.0 |

Identifying Purposes for Reading

Reading and Comprehension

DIRECTIONS: Read each passage and answer the questions.

Lunch Guests

It was a sunny spring day. Kaye and her friend, Tasha, were walking in the woods. As they walked, they noticed many squirrels ahead of them running in the same direction.

"Let's follow them and see where they are going," said Tasha.

"Great idea!" exclaimed Kaye, and the two girls raced ahead.

Soon, they came to a large clearing in the forest. There were hundreds and hundreds of squirrels—more squirrels than either girl had ever seen. As they stared in amazement at the scene before them, a plump gray squirrel with a fluffy tail skittered over to them and said politely, "Would you care to join us for lunch?"

Tasha and Kaye were stunned into silence. But after a moment, they looked at each other, shrugged, and said, "Why not?" They both liked nuts.

Quicksand

Stories of people and animals sinking into quicksand have been told for hundreds of years. Although some of the stories may be true, it helps to understand what quicksand really is.

Quicksand is a deep bed of light, loose sand that is full of water. On the surface, it looks much like regular sand, but it is really very different. Regular sand is packed firmly and can be walked on. Because quicksand is loose and full of water, it cannot support much weight.

Quicksand usually develops around rivers and lakes. Water collects in the sand and does not drain away. It continues to collect until the sand becomes soft.

Although some objects can float in quicksand, it cannot support the heavy weight of an animal or person.

1. **The purpose of the passage about the lunch guests is to _____ .**

   (A) entertain the reader

   (B) alarm the reader

   (C) inform the reader

   (D) challenge the reader

2. **The purpose of the passage about quicksand is to _____ .**

   (F) entertain the reader

   (G) alarm the reader

   (H) inform the reader

   (J) challenge the reader

English Language Arts

1.0

Characteristics of Fiction and Nonfiction
Reading and Comprehension

DIRECTIONS: Read each passage and answer the questions.

Clue

Genre is a type of literature or writing. Some examples of genre include fiction, nonfiction, and poetry.

Dynamite

Dynamite is one of the most powerful explosives in the world. It is often used to blast away earth. This is needed for building dams, making foundations for large buildings, and for mining. The word *dynamite* comes from a Greek word meaning *power.*

Dynamite was first produced in 1867 by Alfred Nobel. Nobel was a Swedish chemist. He later became famous for using his fortune to establish the Nobel Prizes. His first dynamite was dangerous to use because it exploded so easily. He later developed a safer mixture of chemicals and chalk-like soil. He placed this mixture into hollow tubes, or sticks. This stick dynamite was safer because it would not explode until a blasting cap was added. Nobel later invented a special dynamite, called *blasting gelatin*. This dynamite would explode under water.

Today, there are over 200 kinds of dynamite.

1. This passage is which genre of literature?

- (A) fiction
- (B) nonfiction
- (C) biography
- (D) poetry

2. Which of the following is not a characteristic of this genre?

- (F) It tells a story.
- (G) It provides facts.
- (H) It is real and true.
- (J) It informs the reader.

A Bumpy Ride

When we first climbed into the car and strapped on our safety belts, I wasn't very nervous. I was sitting right next to my big brother, and he had done this many times before. As we started to climb the hill, however, I could feel my heart jump into my throat.

"Brian?" I asked nervously. "Is this supposed to be so noisy?"

"Sure, Matthew," Brian answered. "It always does that."

A minute later, we were going so fast down the hill I didn't have time to think. With a twist, a loop, and a bunch of fast turns, everyone on board screamed in delight. No wonder this was one of the most popular rides in the park. By the time the car pulled into the station and we got off the ride, I was ready to do it again!

3. This passage is which genre of literature?

- (A) fiction
- (B) nonfiction
- (C) biography
- (D) poetry

4. Which of the following is not a characteristic of this genre?

- (F) It tells a story.
- (G) It entertains the reader.
- (H) It is not real or true.
- (J) It informs the reader.

STOP

English Language Arts

Interpreting Text
Reading and Comprehension

DIRECTIONS: Read the passage and answer the questions.

The Contest

Tat and Lin loved to enter contests. It did not matter what the prize was. Once, they wrote a poem for a magazine contest. They won a free copy of the magazine. Another time, they guessed how many marbles were in a glass jar. They got to take all the marbles home with them.

One morning, Tat was reading the Crunchy Munchies cereal box as he ate his breakfast. "Lin," he said, "here's another contest! The first-place winner gets a bike. Second prize is a tent."

"Those are great prizes," said Lin. "How do we enter?" The box said that the boys had to fill out a box top with their names and address. The more box tops they filled out, the better their chances for winning the drawing. Tat and Lin started eating Crunchy Munchies every morning. They also asked everyone they knew for cereal box tops.

By the end of four weeks, Tat and Lin had sixteen box tops to send in for the drawing. "I'm glad that's over," said Tat. "If I had to look at another box of that stuff, I don't know what I'd do."

A few weeks passed. One day, the boys got a letter in the mail. "Hooray! We've won third prize in the Crunchy Munchies contest!" Lin exclaimed. "I didn't even know there was a third prize."

Tat took the letter and started to read. His smile disappeared. "Oh, no!" he cried. "Third prize is a year's supply of Crunchy Munchies!"

1. What is this story about?

- (A) two teachers who love cereal
- (B) two cereal makers who love contests
- (C) two sisters who play marbles
- (D) two brothers who love contests

2. How do the boys find out about the Crunchy Munchies contest?

- (F) from a letter in the mail
- (G) from the back of a cereal box
- (H) from their mother
- (J) from their teacher

3. What is the problem in this story?

- (A) Tat and Lin can't figure out how to enter the contest.
- (B) Tat and Lin eat so much cereal they can't stand it anymore.
- (C) Tat and Lin don't collect enough box tops to win.
- (D) Tat and Lin argue about who will get the prize.

4. What do you think Crunchy Munchies is like?

- (F) smooth like pudding
- (G) crisp and sweet
- (H) cooked cereal like oatmeal
- (J) salty like crackers

STOP

English Language Arts

2.0 Identifying Literature Genres
Reading and Comprehension

DIRECTIONS: Each of these passages is a different genre, or type of writing. Read the passages and answer the questions.

The Great Ice Age

Long ago, the climate of the earth began to cool. As the temperature dropped, giant sheets of ice, called *glaciers*, moved across the land. As time went on, snow and ice covered many forests and grasslands.

Some plants and animals could not survive the changes in the climate. Other animals moved to warmer land. But some animals were able to adapt. They learned to live with the cold and snowy weather.

Finally, the earth's temperature began to rise. The ice and snow began to melt. Today, the land at the North and South Poles is a reminder of the Great Ice Age.

Fox and the Grapes

One warm summer day, a fox was walking along when he saw a bunch of grapes on a vine above him. Cool, juicy grapes would taste so good. The more he thought about it, the more the fox wanted those grapes.

He tried standing on his tiptoes. He tried jumping high in the air. He tried getting a running start before he jumped. But no matter what he tried, the fox could not reach the grapes.

As he angrily walked away, the fox muttered, "They were probably sour anyway!"

Moral:

A person (or fox) sometimes pretends that he does not want something he cannot have.

Marie Curie

One of the greatest scientists of all time is Marie Curie. Marie Curie was born in Poland in 1867. She studied at a university in Paris and lived in France for most of her adult life.

Along with her husband, Pierre Curie, she studied radioactivity. She was awarded the Nobel Prize in chemistry in 1911 for her work discovering radium and polonium. Some medical advances are based on the research of the Curies. They include the X-ray and the use of radiation to treat cancer.

The Curies were both generous people. Even though they were poor for most of their lives, they did not patent, or keep the rights to any of their discoveries. They wanted everyone to benefit from their research. Marie Curie died in 1934. The world should not forget her.

Spring Garden

Trees tap at my window
And tell me to come
Out to the garden
Where the wind plays and hums.

Small green buds whisper
Secrets to me
Of spring coming soon
And of flowers yet to be.

I go to the window
And open it wide.
Now the trees shout,
"Please come on outside!"

With a smile on my face,
I race out the door.
I look up at the trees,
Which are swaying once more.

GO

Name _____ Date _____

A **biography** tells the story of a real person's life. A **fable** has a moral, or lesson about how to act. **Nonfiction** includes facts or tells a true story. A **poem** often has rhyming words.

1. **Which of the passages would you classify as a biography?**

   (A) The Great Ice Age

   (B) Marie Curie

   (C) Fox and the Grapes

   (D) Spring Garden

2. **Which of the passages would you classify as a fable?**

   (F) The Great Ice Age

   (G) Marie Curie

   (H) Fox and the Grapes

   (J) Spring Garden

3. **Which of the passages would you classify as nonfiction?**

   (A) The Great Ice Age

   (B) Marie Curie

   (C) Fox and the Grapes

   (D) Spring Garden

4. **Which of the passages would you classify as a poem?**

   (F) The Great Ice Age

   (G) Marie Curie

   (H) Fox and the Grapes

   (J) Spring Garden

5. **What genre, or type of writing, do you like the best? Explain your answer.**

   _____

   _____

   _____

   _____

   _____

   _____

   _____

   _____

   _____

   _____

   _____

   _____

   _____

   _____

   _____

   _____

English Language Arts

2.0

Understanding Works of Literature

Reading and Comprehension

DIRECTIONS: Read the passages and answer the questions.

**paraphrased from *Black Beauty*
by Anna Sewell**

One day, when there was a good deal of kicking in the meadow, my mother whinnied to me to come to her. "I wish you to pay attention to what I am about to say. The colts who live here are very good colts, but they are cart-horse colts, and, of course, they have not learned manners. You have been well-bred and wellborn; your father has a great name in these parts. Your grandfather won the cup two years in a row at the Newmarket Races; your grandmother had the sweetest temper of any horse I have ever known. I think you have never seen me kick or bite. I hope you will grow up gentle and good and never follow bad ways. Do your work with goodwill, lift your legs up high when you trot, and never kick or bite, even in play."

Clue In this passage, "the cup" is a kind of horse race and "temper" means the personality of the horse.

1. **What did Black Beauty's mother say about each of his family members to prove he was "well-bred and wellborn"?**

   A. His father _____
   _____

   B. His grandfather_____
   _____

   C. His grandmother _____
   _____

   D. His mother_____
   _____

2. **In your own words, write what you think "well-bred and wellborn" means.**

   _____

   _____

   _____

   _____

3. **Select the word that best describes the attitude of Black Beauty's mother.**

   Ⓕ proud
   Ⓖ angry
   Ⓗ sad
   Ⓙ carefree

English Language Arts

3.0

Word Meanings
Reading and Comprehension

DIRECTIONS: Read each item. Choose the answer that means the same or about the same as the underlined word.

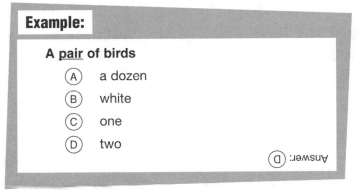

Example:

A <u>pair</u> of birds

Ⓐ a dozen

Ⓑ white

Ⓒ one

Ⓓ two

Answer: (D)

Clue

Your first answer choice is probably correct. Don't change it unless you are sure another answer is better.

1. **A secret <u>bond</u>**

   Ⓐ tie
   Ⓑ search
   Ⓒ trap
   Ⓓ light

2. **<u>Attend</u> a class**

   Ⓕ skip
   Ⓖ pass
   Ⓗ like
   Ⓙ go to

3. **A <u>prize</u> pig**

   Ⓐ award-winning
   Ⓑ clever
   Ⓒ pink
   Ⓓ bad

4. **<u>Towering</u> cliff**

   Ⓕ tipping over
   Ⓖ handmade
   Ⓗ high
   Ⓙ low

DIRECTIONS: Choose the best answer.

5. *To shoplift* is to _____ .

   Ⓐ buy
   Ⓑ steal
   Ⓒ weigh
   Ⓓ walk

6. **A basement is like a** _____ .

   Ⓕ staircase
   Ⓖ attic
   Ⓗ kitchen
   Ⓙ cellar

7. *To faint* is to _____ .

   Ⓐ bow
   Ⓑ wake up
   Ⓒ pass out
   Ⓓ pretend

8. *To be disturbed* is to be _____ .

   Ⓕ noisy
   Ⓖ calm
   Ⓗ joyful
   Ⓙ upset

English Language Arts

3.0

Decoding Strategies
Reading and Comprehension

DIRECTIONS: Find the word that means the same as the underlined word.

1. Tara's <u>excuse</u> was a good one.
   Excuse means _____ .
   - (A) dismiss
   - (B) forgive
   - (C) explanation
   - (D) forgotten

2. The dog seemed <u>fearless</u> as it raced into the crashing waves.
   Fearless means _____ .
   - (F) happy
   - (G) sincere
   - (H) angry
   - (J) unafraid

3. The house was heated by <u>solar</u> energy.
   Solar means _____ .
   - (A) electric
   - (B) water
   - (C) sun-powered
   - (D) gas

4. The roofer used an <u>extension</u> ladder to fix the shingles.
   Extension means _____ .
   - (F) rolling
   - (G) expandable
   - (H) heavy
   - (J) permanent

DIRECTIONS: Find the sentence that uses the underlined word in the same way.

5. The <u>field</u> is planted with corn.
   - (A) The field of technology is constantly changing.
   - (B) We can see deer in the field by our house.
   - (C) Her field is nursing.
   - (D) Our field trip is next Thursday.

6. The <u>general</u> idea was to weave a basket.
   - (F) She is a general in the army.
   - (G) The soldiers followed their general into battle.
   - (H) I think that the general had the best idea.
   - (J) No general study of history can cover everything.

7. Brake pads are made at a <u>plant</u> in our city.
   - (A) The most beautiful plant is a rose.
   - (B) Plant your feet and don't move.
   - (C) Farmers plant crops.
   - (D) My uncle worked at the plant.

Name _____ Date _____

3.0 Defining Words in Context
Reading and Comprehension

DIRECTIONS: Look at the underlined phrases in the passage. Decide what is being described in the phrase by looking at the words around it. Then, answer the questions.

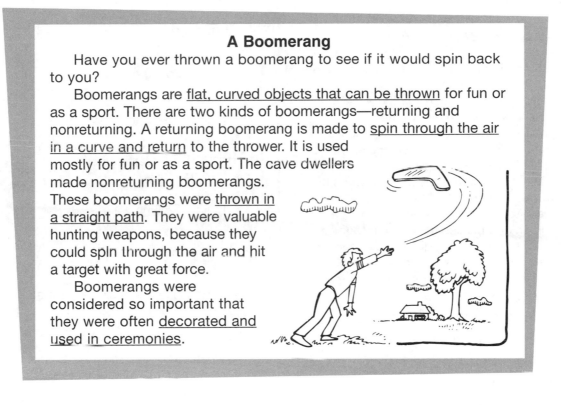

A Boomerang

Have you ever thrown a boomerang to see if it would spin back to you?

Boomerangs are <u>flat, curved objects that can be thrown</u> for fun or as a sport. There are two kinds of boomerangs—returning and nonreturning. A returning boomerang is made to <u>spin through the air in a curve and return</u> to the thrower. It is used mostly for fun or as a sport. The cave dwellers made nonreturning boomerangs. These boomerangs were <u>thrown in a straight path</u>. They were valuable hunting weapons, because they could spin through the air and hit a target with great force.

Boomerangs were considered so important that they were often <u>decorated and used</u> in ceremonies.

1. To what does <u>flat, curved objects that can be thrown</u> refer?
   - (A) cave dwellers
   - (B) scientists
   - (C) boomerangs
   - (D) sport

2. To what does <u>spin through the air in a curve and return</u> refer?
   - (F) fun or sport
   - (G) straight path
   - (H) nonreturning boomerang
   - (J) returning boomerang

3. To what does <u>thrown in a straight path</u> refer?
   - (A) nonreturning boomerang
   - (B) returning boomerang
   - (C) cave dwellers
   - (D) hunting weapons

4. To what does <u>decorated and used in ceremonies</u> refer?
   - (F) boomerangs
   - (G) important
   - (H) stick
   - (J) stone

Name _____   Date _____

Mini-Test 1

Reading and Comprehension

DIRECTIONS: Read the passage and answer the questions.

The Fence
from *The Adventures of Tom Sawyer*
by Mark Twain

Saturday morning was come, and all the summer world was bright and fresh, and brimming with life. There was a song in every heart . . . there was cheer in every face and a spring in every step.

Tom appeared on the sidewalk with a bucket of whitewash and a long-handled brush. He surveyed the fence, and all gladness left him and a deep sadness settled down on his spirit. Thirty yards of board fence nine feet high. Life to him seemed hollow, and existence but a burden. Sighing, he dipped his brush and passed it along the topmost plank; repeated the operation; did it again; compared the small streak with the far-reaching continent of fence, and sat down on a tree-box discouraged.

1. **What is the main problem in the story?**
   - (A) Tom did not know how to sing.
   - (B) Tom needed another bucket.
   - (C) Tom's brush was not long enough.
   - (D) Tom did not want to paint the fence.

2. **This passage is which genre of literature?**
   - (F) poetry
   - (G) fiction
   - (H) biography
   - (J) nonfiction

DIRECTIONS: Choose the answer that means the same as the underlined word.

3. **Thrilling ride**
   - (A) long
   - (B) boring
   - (C) exciting
   - (D) interesting

4. **Dishonest advertisement**
   - (F) trustworthy
   - (G) imaginary
   - (H) true
   - (J) false

DIRECTIONS: Read the passage, then answer the questions.

A Microscope

Have you ever looked into a microscope? A microscope is an <u>instrument</u> that helps us see very small things by <u>magnifying</u> them. Scientists and doctors can use microscopes to study parts of the body, such as blood and skin cells. They can also study germs, tiny plants, and tiny animals.

5. **In this passage, what does the word *instrument* mean?**
   - (A) a tool
   - (B) a drum
   - (C) an office
   - (D) a paper

6. **In this passage, what does the word *magnifying* mean?**
   - (F) making them smaller
   - (G) making them larger
   - (H) making them red
   - (J) making them disappear

Name _____ Date _____

English Language Arts

4.0

Vocabulary Development
Writing

Clue   The meaning of the sentence will give you a clue about which answer to choose.

DIRECTIONS: Choose the word that best fits in the blank.

1. **My mother used the garden _____ to wash the dog.**
   - (A) rake
   - (B) seeds
   - (C) hose
   - (D) gate

2. **The _____ ride on the roller coaster made us yell out loud.**
   - (F) interesting
   - (G) boring
   - (H) slow
   - (J) thrilling

3. **The stormy weather will _____ all night.**
   - (A) change
   - (B) continue
   - (C) stop
   - (D) knock

4. **You should _____ this idea.**
   - (F) think
   - (G) drive
   - (H) consider
   - (J) write

DIRECTIONS: Find the word that means the same as the underlined word.

5. **Are you starting on your <u>journey</u>?**
   ***Journey* means—**
   - (A) class
   - (B) lesson
   - (C) trip
   - (D) vacation

6. **Please bring me <u>Volume</u> K of the encyclopedia.**
   ***Volume* means—**
   - (F) amount
   - (G) book
   - (H) measurement
   - (J) large

7. **His grades have <u>improved</u>.**
   ***Improved* means—**
   - (A) gotten better
   - (B) gotten worse
   - (C) fixed
   - (D) dropped

English Language Arts

4.0

Understanding Point of View
Writing

DIRECTIONS: Read the passages and then answer the questions.

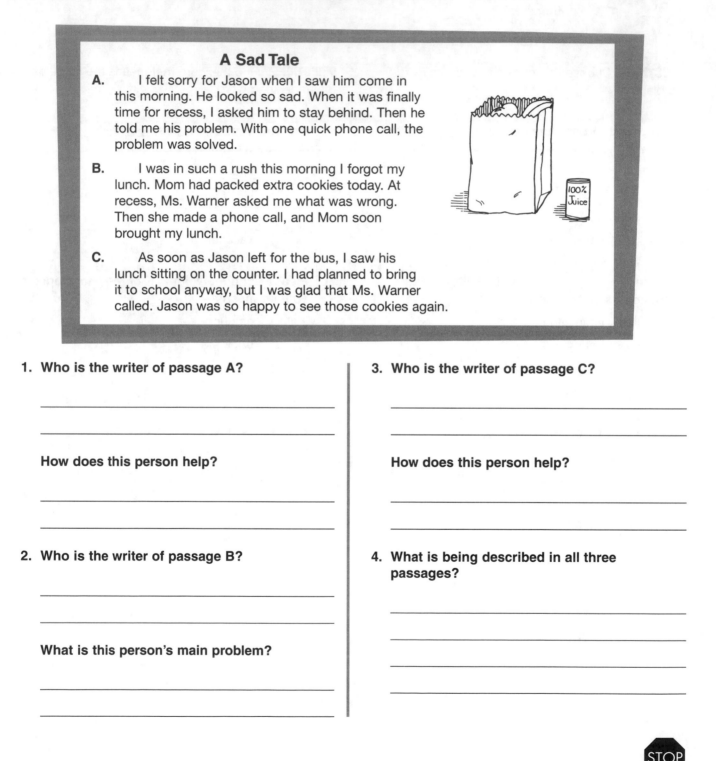

A Sad Tale

A.   I felt sorry for Jason when I saw him come in this morning. He looked so sad. When it was finally time for recess, I asked him to stay behind. Then he told me his problem. With one quick phone call, the problem was solved.

B.   I was in such a rush this morning I forgot my lunch. Mom had packed extra cookies today. At recess, Ms. Warner asked me what was wrong. Then she made a phone call, and Mom soon brought my lunch.

C.   As soon as Jason left for the bus, I saw his lunch sitting on the counter. I had planned to bring it to school anyway, but I was glad that Ms. Warner called. Jason was so happy to see those cookies again.

1. **Who is the writer of passage A?**

_____

_____

How does this person help?

_____

_____

2. **Who is the writer of passage B?**

_____

_____

What is this person's main problem?

_____

_____

3. **Who is the writer of passage C?**

_____

_____

How does this person help?

_____

_____

4. **What is being described in all three passages?**

_____

_____

_____

_____

STOP

Name _____   Date _____

English Language Arts

Identifying Story Elements
Writing

DIRECTIONS: Read the short story about a friend's visit. Then, answer each question below.

> Juan looked at the clock. He paced across the floor. His best friend, Bill, was coming to visit for the first time in six months. Bill had moved very far away. Juan wondered if they would still feel like good friends.
>
> The doorbell rang, and Juan raced to answer it. Bill looked a bit unsure. Juan smiled and started talking just as he always had when they had lived near one another. He made Bill feel comfortable. As the day went on, it felt like old times.

The way a writer describes how a character is acting can give you clues about how the character is feeling.

1. **Who are the main characters in this story?**

   _____

   _____

2. **Where does the story take place?**

   _____

   _____

3. **When does the story take place? Now? In the past? In the future?**

   _____

   _____

   _____

4. **What problem does Juan have?**

   _____

   _____

   _____

5. **What clues in the story helped you to understand how Juan is feeling?**

   _____

   _____

   _____

   _____

   _____

   _____

6. **How does Juan try to solve his problem?**

   _____

   _____

   _____

   _____

   _____

English Language Arts

5.0

Selecting Writing Formats
Writing

DIRECTIONS: Read the paragraph about one student's favorite class. Then, write sentences to answer each question about your favorite class.

> My favorite class is art. I like to draw, and I like to paint. The teacher is very nice. He shows us how to do new things. I always look forward to this class. It would be even better if it were longer.

1. What is your favorite class?

_____

_____

_____

_____

2. Why is it your favorite?

_____

_____

_____

_____

3. Choose one of the following forms of writing—poem, story, or letter—to describe your ideas and feelings about your favorite class. Identify who your audience will be before writing.

_____

_____

_____

_____

_____

_____

_____

_____

_____

_____

_____

_____

_____

_____

Name _____ Date _____

5.0

Writing With Organization
Writing

DIRECTIONS: Write a paragraph about one of your favorite activities. Make sure your paragraph has a main idea and details that support the main idea. Use the chart below to create a rough draft of your paragraph. Then, write the final paragraph on the lines below.

Main Idea:	
Detail #1:	
Detail #2:	
Detail #3:	
Detail #4:	
Conclusion:	

_____

_____

_____

_____

_____

_____

_____

_____

_____

English Language Arts

5.0

Beginnings, Middles, and Ends

Writing

DIRECTIONS: Read the passage and answer the questions.

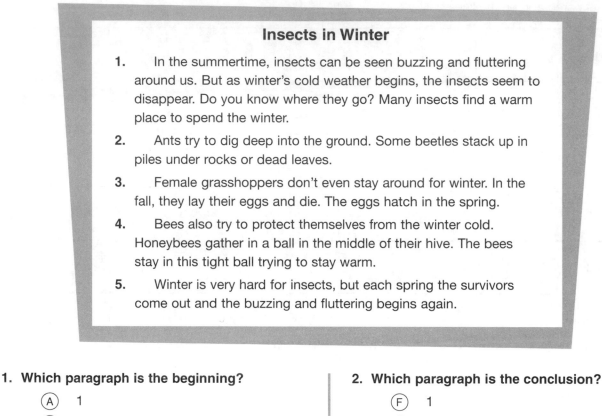

Insects in Winter

1.   In the summertime, insects can be seen buzzing and fluttering around us. But as winter's cold weather begins, the insects seem to disappear. Do you know where they go? Many insects find a warm place to spend the winter.

2.   Ants try to dig deep into the ground. Some beetles stack up in piles under rocks or dead leaves.

3.   Female grasshoppers don't even stay around for winter. In the fall, they lay their eggs and die. The eggs hatch in the spring.

4.   Bees also try to protect themselves from the winter cold. Honeybees gather in a ball in the middle of their hive. The bees stay in this tight ball trying to stay warm.

5.   Winter is very hard for insects, but each spring the survivors come out and the buzzing and fluttering begins again.

1. **Which paragraph is the beginning?**
    (A) 1
    (B) 2
    (C) 3
    (D) 5

2. **Which paragraph is the conclusion?**
    (F) 1
    (G) 2
    (H) 4
    (J) 5

3. **Use the passage to fill in the topic sentence below. Fill in the rest of the ovals with supporting details.**

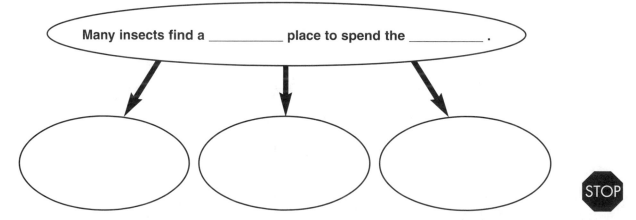

Many insects find a _____ place to spend the _____ .

English Language Arts

| 5.0/6.0 | # Using Writing Structures |

Writing

DIRECTIONS: Read the paragraph that tells how to make a peanut butter and jelly sandwich. Then, think of something you like to make or do. Write a paragraph that tells how to make it. Use the words *first, next, then,* and *last* to show the transition between steps.

These steps tell how to make a peanut butter and jelly sandwich. First, get two pieces of bread, peanut butter, jelly, and a knife. Next, spread peanut butter on one piece of bread. Then, spread jelly on the other piece. Last, press the two pieces of bread together.

1. _____

_____

_____

_____

_____

_____

_____

_____

_____

_____

_____

_____

_____

_____

_____

_____

DIRECTIONS: Read the paragraph below about how to make a peanut butter and jelly sandwich. Notice that the steps are now numbered. In the space below, rewrite your directions for number 1. This time, use numbered steps instead of transitional words.

These steps tell how to make a peanut butter and jelly sandwich.
1. Get two pieces of bread, peanut butter, jelly, and a knife.
2. Spread peanut butter on one piece of bread.
3. Spread jelly on the other piece.
4. Press the two pieces of bread together.

2. _____

_____

_____

_____

_____

_____

_____

_____

_____

_____

_____

_____

_____

_____

STOP

English Language Arts

6.0

Spelling
Writing

DIRECTIONS: For numbers 1–6, find the underlined word that is not spelled correctly. If all of the words are spelled correctly, choose "all correct."

1. (A) <u>identify</u> a bird
    (B) bottle of <u>juice</u>
    (C) <u>quiet</u> room
    (D) all correct

2. (F) easy <u>lesson</u>
    (G) bright <u>lites</u>
    (H) <u>paddle</u> a canoe
    (J) all correct

3. (A) good <u>balance</u>
    (B) <u>runing</u> shoes
    (C) <u>private</u> property
    (D) all correct

4. (F) great <u>relief</u>
    (G) our <u>house</u>
    (H) <u>sunnie</u> day
    (J) all correct

5. (A) <u>forty</u> years
    (B) <u>twelve</u> pears
    (C) a <u>thousend</u> questions
    (D) all correct

6. (F) my <u>brother</u>
    (G) your <u>friend</u>
    (H) his <u>uncle</u>
    (J) all correct

DIRECTIONS: For numbers 7–11, find the word that is spelled correctly and fits best in the blank.

7. We opened the _____ .
    (A) presence
    (B) presants
    (C) presents
    (D) prasents

8. We picked _____ in our garden.
    (F) berries
    (G) berrys
    (H) berrese
    (J) berreis

9. The _____ helped me.
    (A) nourse
    (B) nurce
    (C) nirse
    (D) nurse

10. The answer to this problem is a _____ .
    (F) frackshun
    (G) fracteon
    (H) fraction
    (J) fracton

11. Did you _____ the page?
    (A) tare
    (B) tair
    (C) tear
    (D) taer

Name _____ Date _____

6.0 # Capitalization and Punctuation
Writing

Clue Remember that sentences and proper nouns start with capital letters.

DIRECTIONS: For numbers 1–3, choose the answer that has a missing capital letter. If no capital letters are missing, choose the answer "none."

1.
(A) I want
(B) to read the book
(C) *The Light in the window.*
(D) none

2.
(F) Oliver knows
(G) he isn't
(H) supposed to do that.
(J) none

3.
(A) did you
(B) find your gift
(C) on the table?
(D) none

DIRECTIONS: For numbers 4 and 5, choose the answer that has the correct capitalization.

4. **The ruler of England at that time was _____ .**
(F) king George I
(G) King George I
(H) king george I
(J) King george I

5. **The bus arrived at _____ more than three hours late.**
(A) the Station
(B) The station
(C) The Station
(D) the station

DIRECTIONS: For numbers 6–9, choose the answer that shows the correct punctuation.

6. **The cake _____ in the oven.**
(F) wasn't
(G) wasn't'
(H) wasnt
(J) was'nt

7. **_____ starting to snow!**
(A) Its
(B) I'ts
(C) It's
(D) Its'

8.
(F) You will need some paper a pencil and an eraser.
(G) You will need some paper, a pencil and, an eraser.
(H) You will need some paper; a pencil; and an eraser.
(J) You will need some paper, a pencil, and an eraser

9.
(A) Michael's grandmother gave him a puppy.
(B) Michaels grandmother gave him a puppy.
(C) Michaels' grandmother gave him a puppy.
(D) Michael's grandmother's gave him a puppy.

Name _____ Date _____

English Language Arts

6.0

Subject and Verb Agreement

Writing

DIRECTIONS: Choose the answer that best completes the sentence.

1. **Chang and Audrey made _____ kites together.**
   - (A) him
   - (B) she
   - (C) they
   - (D) their

2. **Are _____ parents coming to the concert?**
   - (F) she
   - (G) he
   - (H) her
   - (J) it

3. **_____ spoke to my mother on Parents' Night.**
   - (A) Him
   - (B) He
   - (C) Us
   - (D) Them

DIRECTIONS: Choose the answer that could replace the underlined word.

4. **Tyrone has a baseball card collection.**
   - (F) Him
   - (G) He
   - (H) We
   - (J) Them

5. **Jill and Keisha went to soccer practice.**
   - (A) Him
   - (B) Them
   - (C) They
   - (D) She

6. **I thought the play was very good.**
   - (F) him
   - (G) her
   - (H) we
   - (J) it

DIRECTIONS: Choose the answer that uses an incorrect verb.

7. (A) The skipper steering the boat.
   - (B) The wind blew across the lake.
   - (C) The boat stayed on course.
   - (D) The brave skipper brought the boat safely to shore.

8. (F) The dentist cleaned my teeth.
   - (G) I was worried he might have to use the drill.
   - (H) He were very nice.
   - (J) My teeth are shiny now!

9. (A) The pioneer chose his land carefully.
   - (B) He wanted a stream near his cabin.
   - (C) He wanting good land for crops.
   - (D) He knew he could use the trees for building.

STOP

English Language Arts

| 4.0–6.0 |

For pages 19–28

Mini-Test 2

Writing

DIRECTIONS: Read the paragraph, and answer the questions.

Before Samantha woke up, I left her presents beside her bed. I knew she would like the surprise from her father and me. When we saw Samantha on the stairs, we surprised her by saying, "Happy birthday!"

1. **Who is the writer of the paragraph?**
   - (A) Samantha
   - (B) Samantha's mom
   - (C) Samantha's sister
   - (D) Samantha's dad

2. **What clue helped you identify the writer?**

   _____

   _____

   _____

DIRECTIONS: Find the underlined word that is not spelled correctly.

3.
   - (F) my <u>favorite</u> food
   - (G) writing <u>journel</u>
   - (H) best <u>friends</u>
   - (J) all correct

4.
   - (A) <u>beutiful</u> house
   - (B) <u>exciting</u> day
   - (C) <u>write</u> with a pen
   - (D) all correct

DIRECTIONS: Choose the answer that shows the correct punctuation and capitalization.

5.
   - (F) What is your favorite city
   - (G) I like San francisco.
   - (H) It's in California.
   - (J) The golden gate Bridge is in San francisco.

6.
   - (A) October, 12, 2006
   - (B) october 12, 2006
   - (C) October 12, 2006
   - (D) October 12 2006

7. **Choose the answer that uses an incorrect verb.**
   - (F) The spider spun a beautiful web.
   - (G) Dew glistened on it in the morning.
   - (H) The spider wait to catch a fly.
   - (J) I'm glad the spider is outside.

8. **Choose the sentence that is written correctly.**
   - (A) Concert in the park last night.
   - (B) Music, dancing, and cheering.
   - (C) Over a thousand people was there.
   - (D) I will never forget that concert.

Name _____ Date _____

Generating Ideas
Research

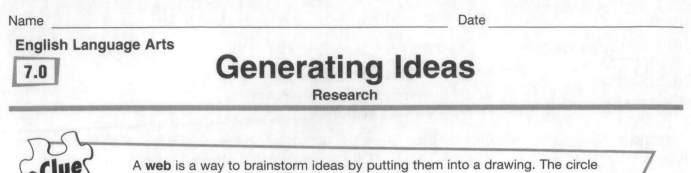 A **web** is a way to brainstorm ideas by putting them into a drawing. The circle in the middle shows the main topic. The other circles contain ideas about the main topic.

Here is an example of a web about cats. All of the ideas that are related to cats are connected to the circle in the middle. Sometimes those ideas make you think of other things. For example, the main topic of cats can make you think about lions, so you add a circle for that idea. Then lions can make you think about their home in Africa, so you add another circle connected to lions. Keep adding circles as you think of new ideas that relate to the main topic.

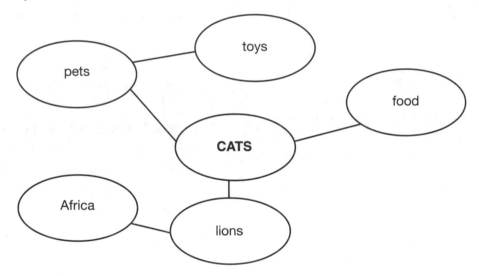

DIRECTIONS: Now, pick a topic of your own and brainstorm a web. Draw lines to connect any ideas that are related.

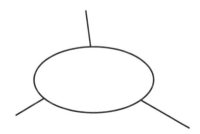

English Language Arts

8.0

Using Classroom Resources

Research

DIRECTIONS: Read numbers 1–11. Then, choose where this information is most likely to be found. Write the letter for each answer choice on the blank lines.

   A. in an atlas

   B. in a dictionary

   C. in an encyclopedia

   D. in a newspaper

1. _____ **pronunciation of a word**

2. _____ **types of animals in a rain forest**

3. _____ **map of Pennsylvania**

4. _____ **comic strip**

5. _____ **place where Abraham Lincoln was born**

6. _____ **report of a fire in your neighborhood**

7. _____ **definition of the word** *concave*

8. _____ **latitude and longitude of Paris, France**

9. _____ **local job listings**

10. _____ **the date that World War II ended**

11. _____ **how to break a word into syllables**

DIRECTIONS: Read the following paragraph. Then, choose the best answer.

What I remember most about that big old house in Iowa was the kitchen, a room that was always warm and smelled wonderful.

12. **This sentence would most likely be found in _____ .**

   Ⓐ a newspaper article

   Ⓑ an autobiography

   Ⓒ an encyclopedia

   Ⓓ a science book

13. **Which of these sentences would most likely be found in a newspaper article?**

   Ⓕ "Now hold on there," said the sheriff. "We don't put up with things like that in this town."

   Ⓖ It wasn't a star they were looking at, but a spaceship, and it was coming right at them.

   Ⓗ Guido said good-bye to his family, picked up his bags, and joined the crowd walking toward the ship.

   Ⓙ A recent report from the school board stated that there are more students in our school than there were last year.

GO

Name _____   Date _____

 Clue   Remember, a table of contents gives you the names of chapters or topics in a book, and an index shows you where specific information is found.

DIRECTIONS: Read the table of contents and index. Then, answer the questions.

TABLE OF CONTENTS

INDEX

14. Chapter 2 begins on page _____ .

(A) 11
(B) 42
(C) 59
(D) 85

15. Which chapter starts on page 59?

(F) Insects and Spiders
(G) Rodents
(H) Creatures of the Sea
(J) Zoos of the World

16. To find out about rain forest animals, turn to pages _____ .

(A) 60–64
(B) 103–107
(C) 39–41
(D) 14–15

17. Which chapter would you read to learn about rats?

(F) Chapter 1
(G) Chapter 2
(H) Chapter 3
(J) Chapter 4

18. If you wanted information on blue whales, you would turn to page _____ .

(A) 60
(B) 61
(C) 62
(D) 64

19. Look at the guide words for a dictionary. Which word would be found on this page?

(F) empire
(G) enchant
(H) engrave
(J) enter

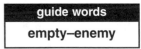

guide words
empty–enemy

DIRECTIONS: Choose the best answer.

20. Which word comes first in the dictionary?

(A) bless
(B) belt
(C) bear
(D) blue

English Language Arts

| 7.0–8.0 |

For pages 30–32

Mini-Test 3

Research

DIRECTIONS: Choose the best answer.

1. **Where would you look to find information about sharks?**
   - (A) in a newspaper
   - (B) in a history book
   - (C) in a dictionary
   - (D) in an encyclopedia

2. **Where would you look to check the pronunciation of the word** *accept*?
   - (F) in a newspaper
   - (G) in an atlas
   - (H) in a dictionary
   - (J) in an encyclopedia

3. **Where would you look to find information about today's weather forecast?**
   - (A) in a newspaper
   - (B) in an atlas
   - (C) in a dictionary
   - (D) in an encyclopedia

4. **Where would you look to find a map of Georgia?**
   - (F) in a newspaper
   - (G) in an atlas
   - (H) in a dictionary
   - (J) in a math textbook

5. **Where would you look to find information about the fourth president of the United States?**
   - (A) in a newspaper
   - (B) in a magazine
   - (C) in a dictionary
   - (D) in an encyclopedia

6. **Where would you look to check your spelling of the word** *beautiful*?
   - (F) in a dictionary
   - (G) in a newspaper
   - (H) in an atlas
   - (J) in an encyclopedia

7. **Which word comes first in the dictionary?**
   - (A) ditch
   - (B) drink
   - (C) damp
   - (D) deep

8. **Which word comes first in the dictionary?**
   - (F) creek
   - (G) cloud
   - (H) cut
   - (J) car

9. **Which word comes first in the dictionary?**
   - (A) meat
   - (B) mouse
   - (C) make
   - (D) mine

10. **Look at the guide words for a dictionary. Which word would be found on this page?**
    - (F) clock
    - (G) climate
    - (H) clear
    - (J) clog

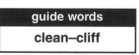

guide words
clean–cliff

STOP

English Language Arts

9.0

Comparing Literature From Different Cultures

Cultural and Social Language Use

DIRECTIONS: Read the following passages taken from different cultures. Then, answer the questions that follow.

Why the Sun and the Moon Live in the Sky

Many, many years ago, the Sun and the Moon lived together on the earth. Water was their best friend, and they often came to see him. But Water never went to see the Sun and the Moon in their house. The Sun asked Water why he didn't visit. Water answered that he had too many friends and was afraid there would be no place for them in his house.

So, the Sun built a very big house and then asked Water to come to him. Water came with all the fish and water animals. Soon, Water was up to the Sun's head and came higher and higher with all the fish and water animals. At last, Water was so high in the house that the Sun and the Moon went to the roof and sat there. Water soon came up onto the roof. What could the Sun and the Moon do? Where could they sit? They went up to the sky. They liked the place and began to live there.

—Ghana folktale

How the Moon and the Stars Came to Be

One day in the times when the sky was close to the ground, a woman went out to pound rice. Before she began her work, she took off the beads from around her neck and the comb from her hair. She hung her comb and beads in the sky. Then, she began working. Each time she raised her pestle into the air to pound the rice, it hit the sky. The sky began to rise. It went up so far that the woman lost her beads and comb. Never did they come back down, for the comb became the moon and the beads became the stars that are scattered about.

—Philippine folktale

1. **What is explained in the first story?**

   _____

   _____

   _____

2. **What is explained in the second story?**

   _____

   _____

3. **These two stories are from different cultures. How are the stories similar to each other?**

   _____

   _____

   _____

   _____

   _____

   _____

Name _____   Date _____

English Language Arts

Sharing Writing With Others
Cultural and Social Language Use

DIRECTIONS: Think about a fictional short story you would like to write. Use the questions below to help you get started. After you answer the questions, write a first draft of your story. Then, read through it and make changes to improve your story.

1. **Think about the main character in your story. Who is it? What is he or she like?**

   _____

   _____

   _____

   _____

2. **Where does the story take place? When does the story take place? Now? In the past? In the future?**

   _____

   _____

   _____

   _____

3. **What problem will the main character(s) have? How will he or she try to solve the problem?**

   _____

   _____

   _____

   _____

4. **What are some details you can include that will make your story interesting to read?**

   _____

   _____

   _____

   _____

5. **After you create your first draft, have another person, such as a classmate or parent, read your short story. Then, have them answer the following questions: What did you like the best about the story? Are there any places where I should make some changes? What other details do you think I should include?**

How Am I Doing?

Mini-Test 1	**6** answers correct	**Great Job!** Move on to the section test on page 40.
Page 18 **Number Correct**	**4–5** answers correct	**You're almost there!** But you still need a little practice. Review practice pages 9–17 before moving on to the section test on page 40.
	0–3 answers correct	**Oops!** Time to review what you have learned and try again. Review the practice section on pages 9–17. Then, retake the test on page 18. Now, move on to the section test on page 40.
Mini-Test 2	**7–8** answers correct	**Awesome!** Move on to the section test on page 40.
Page 29 **Number Correct**	**5–6** answers correct	**You're almost there!** But you still need a little practice. Review practice pages 19–28 before moving on to the section test on page 40.
	0–4 answers correct	**Oops!** Time to review what you have learned and try again. Review the practice section on pages 19–28. Then, retake the test on page 29. Now, move on to the section test on page 40.
Mini-Test 3	**9–10** answers correct	**Great Job!** Move on to the section test on page 40.
Page 33 **Number Correct**	**5–8** answers correct	**You're almost there!** But you still need a little practice. Review practice pages 30–32 before moving on to the section test on page 40.
	0–4 answers correct	**Oops!** Time to review what you have learned and try again. Review the practice section on pages 30–32. Then, retake the test on page 33. Now, move on to the section test on page 40.

How Am I Doing?

Mini-Test 4	3 answers correct	**Awesome!** Move on to the section test on page 40.
Page 37 **Number Correct**	2 answers correct	**You're almost there!** But you still need a little practice. Review practice pages 34–36 before moving on to the section test on page 40.
	0–1 answers correct	**Oops!** Time to review what you have learned and try again. Review the practice section on pages 34–36. Then, retake the test on page 37. Now, move on to the section test on page 40.

Final English Language Arts Test
for pages 9–37

DIRECTIONS: Read the passage and then choose the best answer for each question.

Therapy Dogs

Therapy dogs can help patients get better after illnesses. The dogs' owners bring them into hospital rooms and let patients meet the animals. Dogs sometimes go right up to patients' beds. People in the hospital rooms can pet the dogs, brush them, and talk to them. Studies have shown that being with dogs and other animals is therapeutic. It can lower stress, lower blood pressure, and help people heal faster.

Not every dog is a good choice for this important job. To be a therapy dog, a dog must have a calm, friendly disposition. Some therapy dog owners feel that their pets were born to help sick people get well again.

1. **What is the main idea of this passage?**
    - (A) Therapy dogs like to be brushed.
    - (B) Therapy dogs are calm and friendly.
    - (C) Therapy dogs help patients get better after illnesses.
    - (D) Therapy dogs were born to visit hospitals.

2. **The word *disposition* means _____ .**
    - (F) work history
    - (G) personality
    - (H) intelligence
    - (J) breed

3. **Which words help you figure out the meaning of *therapeutic*?**
    - (A) "sometimes go right up to patients' beds"
    - (B) "lower stress, lower blood pressure, and help people heal faster"
    - (C) "a calm, friendly disposition"
    - (D) "pet the dogs, brush them, and talk to them"

DIRECTIONS: Read the passage. On the next page, choose the best answer for each question.

Wendy, Lost and Found

Wendy was scared. For the second time in her young life, she was lost. When the branch fell on her small house and the fence, she had barely escaped. She had leaped across the fallen fence into the woods. Now, the rain poured down and the wind howled. The little woodchuck shivered under a big oak tree. She did not know what to do.

When Wendy was a baby, her mother died. She had been alone in the woods then, too. She could not find enough food. Then, she hurt her paw. All day, she scratched at a small hole in the ground, trying to make a burrow. Every night, she was hungry.

One day, Rita found her. Rita had knelt down by Wendy's shallow burrow and set down an apple. Wendy limped out slowly and took the apple. It was the best thing she had ever tasted. Rita took the baby woodchuck to the wildlife center, and Wendy has lived there ever since. Most of the animals at the center were orphans. Rita taught them how to live in the wild and then let them go when they were ready. But Wendy's paw did not heal well, and Rita knew that Wendy would never be able to go back to the wild. So, Rita made Wendy a house and a pen. Wendy even had a job—she visited schools with Rita so that students could learn all about woodchucks.

Now, the storm had ruined Wendy's house. She did not know how to find Rita. At dawn, the rain ended. Wendy limped down to a big stream and sniffed the air. Maybe the center was across the stream. Wendy jumped onto a rock and then hopped to another one. She landed on her bad paw and fell into the fast-moving water. The little woodchuck struggled to keep her nose above water. The current tossed her against a tangle of branches. Wendy held on with all her might.

"There she is!" Wendy heard Rita's voice. Rita and Ben, another worker from the wildlife center, were across the stream. Rita waded out to the branches, lifted Wendy up, and wrapped her in a blanket. Wendy purred her thanks. By the time Ben and Rita got into the van to go back to the center, Wendy was fast asleep.

GO

4. What genre of literature is this passage?

- (F) biography
- (G) nonfiction
- (H) fiction
- (J) poetry

5. This passage is mostly about _____ .

- (A) a wildlife center worker
- (B) a woodchuck who lives at a wildlife center
- (C) a woodchuck who can do tricks
- (D) a woodchuck who learns how to swim

6. How does the passage start?

- (F) with Wendy's life as a baby
- (G) in the middle of the storm
- (H) with Wendy's visit to school
- (J) when Wendy is in the stream

7. What are the settings for this passage?

- (A) the woods and the wildlife center
- (B) the school and the stream
- (C) the school and the woods
- (D) the wildlife center and Rita's house

DIRECTIONS: Choose the best answer.

8. Find the answer that means the same or about the same as the underlined word.

long <u>tale</u>

- (F) story
- (G) movie
- (H) road
- (J) trip

9. Find the word that means the opposite of the underlined word.

<u>dull</u> ride

- (A) long
- (B) exciting
- (C) boring
- (D) sad

10. Find the word that fits best in the blank.
Dogs need _____ to stay healthy.

- (F) treats
- (G) dishes
- (H) exercise
- (J) collars

11. Choose the word that correctly completes both sentences.
Who will _____ this problem?
The _____ on the shovel is broken.

- (A) solve
- (B) blade
- (C) cause
- (D) handle

DIRECTIONS: Choose the answer that shows the correct punctuation and capitalization.

12.
- (F) Yesterday, i got a new kitten!
- (G) I named her tara.
- (H) She came from the animal shelter
- (J) She has green eyes and black fur.

13.
- (A) She and i will study now.
- (B) the library is closed.
- (C) Let's leave now?
- (D) May I borrow that book when you're done?

GO

DIRECTIONS: Choose the word that best completes the sentence.

14. Don't _____ in the hallway.

(F) running

(G) ran

(H) run

(J) had run

15. Please lend _____ your mittens.

(A) her

(B) she

(C) its

(D) they

DIRECTIONS: Choose the answer that uses an incorrect verb.

16. (F) The cowboy got on his horse.

(G) He rode quickly away from the cattle.

(H) The lost calf was bleating loudly.

(J) The cowboy taken the calf to its mother.

17. (A) The spider spun a beautiful web.

(B) Dew glistened on it in the morning.

(C) The spider wait to catch a fly.

(D) I'm glad the spider is outside.

DIRECTIONS: Choose the answer that you think is correct.

18. Where would you look to find the date of Memorial Day this year?

(F) in a newspaper

(G) in an encyclopedia

(H) in a dictionary

(J) on a calendar

19. Where would you look to find a biography of Martin Luther King, Jr.?

(A) in a newspaper

(B) in an atlas

(C) in an encyclopedia

(D) in a dictionary

20. Which of these words comes first in the dictionary?

(F) cracker

(G) cup

(H) climb

(J) chalk

DIRECTIONS: Read the table of contents. Then, answer the questions.

TABLE OF CONTENTS

21. To learn how to teach your dog to sit, turn to _____ .

(A) Chapter 1

(B) Chapter 2

(C) Chapter 3

(D) Chapter 4

22. Which chapter starts on page 11?

(F) Choosing Your Breed of Dog

(G) Medical Care for Dogs

(H) Training Young Dogs

(J) Do You Have a Champion?

Final English Language Arts Test

Answer Sheet

1. Ⓐ Ⓑ Ⓒ Ⓓ
2. Ⓕ Ⓖ Ⓗ Ⓙ
3. Ⓐ Ⓑ Ⓒ Ⓓ
4. Ⓕ Ⓖ Ⓗ Ⓙ
5. Ⓐ Ⓑ Ⓒ Ⓓ
6. Ⓕ Ⓖ Ⓗ Ⓙ
7. Ⓐ Ⓑ Ⓒ Ⓓ
8. Ⓕ Ⓖ Ⓗ Ⓙ
9. Ⓐ Ⓑ Ⓒ Ⓓ
10. Ⓕ Ⓖ Ⓗ Ⓙ

11. Ⓐ Ⓑ Ⓒ Ⓓ
12. Ⓕ Ⓖ Ⓗ Ⓙ
13. Ⓐ Ⓑ Ⓒ Ⓓ
14. Ⓕ Ⓖ Ⓗ Ⓙ
15. Ⓐ Ⓑ Ⓒ Ⓓ
16. Ⓕ Ⓖ Ⓗ Ⓙ
17. Ⓐ Ⓑ Ⓒ Ⓓ
18. Ⓕ Ⓖ Ⓗ Ⓙ
19. Ⓐ Ⓑ Ⓒ Ⓓ
20. Ⓕ Ⓖ Ⓗ Ⓙ

21. Ⓐ Ⓑ Ⓒ Ⓓ
22. Ⓕ Ⓖ Ⓗ Ⓙ

Mathematics Standards

Standard 1—Number and Operations *(See pages 45–49.)*
  A. Understand numbers, ways of representing numbers, relationships among numbers, and number systems.
  B. Understand meanings of operations and how they relate to one another.
  C. Compute fluently and make reasonable estimates.

Standard 2—Algebra *(See pages 50–53.)*
  A. Understand patterns, relations, and functions.
  B. Represent and analyze mathematical situations and structures using algebraic symbols.
  C. Use mathematical models to represent and understand quantitative relationships.
  D. Analyze change in various contexts.

Standard 3—Geometry *(See pages 55–60.)*
  A. Analyze characteristics and properties of two- and three-dimensional shapes and develop mathematical arguments about geometric relationships.
  B. Specify locations and describe spatial relationships using coordinate geometry and other representational systems.
  C. Apply transformations and use symmetry to analyze mathematical situations.
  D. Use visualization, spatial reasoning, and geometric modeling to solve problems.

Standard 4—Measurement *(See pages 61–64.)*
  A. Understand measurable attributes of objects and the units, systems, and processes of measurement.
  B. Apply appropriate techniques, tools, and formulas to determine measurement.

Standard 5—Data Analysis and Probability *(See pages 66–68.)*
  A. Formulate questions that can be addressed with data and collect, organize, and display relevant data to answer them.
  B. Select and use appropriate statistical methods to analyze data.
  C. Develop and evaluate inferences and predictions that are based on data.
  D. Understand and apply basic concepts of probability.

Standard 6—Process *(See pages 69–72.)*
  A. Problem Solving
  B. Reasoning and Proof
  C. Communication
  D. Connections
  E. Representation

1.A

Using Whole Numbers
Number and Operations

DIRECTIONS: Choose the best answer.

1. If you arranged these numbers from least to greatest, which number would be last?

   1,012   1,022   1,002   1,021

   (A)   1,012
   (B)   1,021
   (C)   1,022
   (D)   1,002

2. Which of these numbers would come before 157 on a number line?

   (F)   159
   (G)   147
   (H)   165
   (J)   158

3. Which of these numbers is nine hundred sixty-four?

   (A)   9,604
   (B)   946
   (C)   9,640
   (D)   964

4. Which group of numbers has three odd numbers?

   (F)   8, 12, 15, 17, 20, 26, 30
   (G)   7, 10, 12, 13, 19, 22, 36
   (H)   2, 5, 8, 14, 18, 28, 32, 40
   (J)   16, 27, 28, 29, 30, 34, 38

5. Which of these is closest in value to 190?

   (A)   186
   (B)   192
   (C)   179
   (D)   199

6. Paul and Vesta used a computer to solve a problem. Which of these is the same as the number on the screen?

   (F)   three thousand one hundred eighty
   (G)   three hundred eighty
   (H)   three thousand one hundred eight
   (J)   three thousand eighteen

7. Count by fives. Which number comes after 25 and before 35?

   (A)   50
   (B)   20
   (C)   30
   (D)   40

8. Which of these numbers is eight hundred one thousand, three hundred twenty-two?

   (F)   810,322
   (G)   800,322
   (H)   801,322
   (J)   813,220

9. Which of these is closest in value to 503,561?

   (A)   504,561
   (B)   502,561
   (C)   503,651
   (D)   503,165

Mathematics

1.A

Composing and Decomposing Numbers

Number and Operations

DIRECTIONS: Choose the best answer.

Read the questions carefully. Try to think of an answer before you look at the answers.

1. **How can you write 56,890 in expanded notation?**

   Ⓐ 5 + 6 + 8 + 9 + 0

   Ⓑ 50,000 + 6,000 + 800 + 90

   Ⓒ 56,000 + 8,900

   Ⓓ 0.5 + 0.06 + 0.008 + 0.0009

2. **What is another name for 651?**

   Ⓕ 6 thousands, 5 tens, and 1 one

   Ⓖ 6 hundreds, 1 ten, and 5 ones

   Ⓗ 6 tens and 5 ones

   Ⓙ 6 hundreds, 5 tens, and 1 one

3. **7 thousands and 5 hundreds equals _____ .**

   Ⓐ 5,700

   Ⓑ 7,050

   Ⓒ 570

   Ⓓ 7,500

4. **What is another name for 8 hundreds, 4 tens, and 3 ones?**

   Ⓕ 8,430

   Ⓖ 843

   Ⓗ 834

   Ⓙ 8,043

5. **What is another name for 4 hundreds, 6 tens, and 5 ones?**

   Ⓐ 4,650

   Ⓑ 465

   Ⓒ 40,650

   Ⓓ 4,560

6. **How can you write 9,876 in expanded notation?**

   Ⓕ 9,800 + 76 + 0

   Ⓖ 9,800 + 70 + 60

   Ⓗ 9,000 + 870 + 60

   Ⓙ 9,000 + 800 + 70 + 6

7. **What number equals 4 thousands, 2 hundreds, 2 tens, and 2 ones?**

   Ⓐ 4,202

   Ⓑ 4,200

   Ⓒ 4,022

   Ⓓ 4,222

8. **How many tens are in 60?**

   Ⓕ 6

   Ⓖ 10

   Ⓗ 1

   Ⓙ 0

STOP

Relating Multiplication and Division

Number and Operations

DIRECTIONS: Choose the best answer.

1. $32 \div 16 = 2$; $16 \times \blacksquare = 32$
   - (A) 32
   - (B) 16
   - (C) 2
   - (D) 8

2. $25 \div 5 = \blacksquare$; $5 \times \blacksquare = 25$
   - (F) 5
   - (G) 25
   - (H) 50
   - (J) 10

3. $81 \div 9 = \blacksquare$; $9 \times \blacksquare = 81$
   - (A) 3
   - (B) 81
   - (C) 12
   - (D) 9

4. $144 \div 12 = \blacksquare$; $12 \times \blacksquare = 144$
   - (F) 48
   - (G) 14
   - (H) 24
   - (J) 12

5. $56 \div 14 = \blacksquare$; $14 \times \blacksquare = 56$
   - (A) 6
   - (B) 4
   - (C) 8
   - (D) 9

6. $64 \div 8 = \blacksquare$; $8 \times \blacksquare = 64$
   - (F) 9
   - (G) 8
   - (H) 12
   - (J) 56

7. $3 \times \blacksquare = 27$; $27 \div \blacksquare = 3$
   - (A) 3
   - (B) 27
   - (C) 9
   - (D) 8

8. $7 \times \blacksquare = 56$; $56 \div 7 = \blacksquare$
   - (F) 8
   - (G) 9
   - (H) 14
   - (J) 28

9. $13 \times 3 = \blacksquare$; $\blacksquare \div 3 = 13$
   - (A) 16
   - (B) 26
   - (C) 39
   - (D) 52

10. $11 \times \blacksquare = 121$; $121 \div \blacksquare = 11$
    - (F) 10
    - (G) 11
    - (H) 12
    - (J) 13

Mathematics

1.B

Multiplying and Dividing

Number and Operations

DIRECTIONS: Choose the best answer.

Clue Skim the problems and do the easiest ones first. Check your answer using the opposite operation.

1. $6 \times 4 =$
   - (A) 18
   - (B) 24
   - (C) 21
   - (D) 32

2. $9 \times 6 =$
   - (F) 54
   - (G) 49
   - (H) 63
   - (J) 52

3. $7 \times 8 =$
   - (A) 56
   - (B) 64
   - (C) 63
   - (D) 49

4. $5 \times 9 =$
   - (F) 40
   - (G) 55
   - (H) 45
   - (J) 42

5. $3 \times 6 =$
   - (A) 12
   - (B) 15
   - (C) 21
   - (D) 18

6. $100 \div 10 =$
   - (F) 10
   - (G) 100
   - (H) 1
   - (J) none of these

7. $426 \div 6 =$
   - (A) 61
   - (B) 51
   - (C) 71
   - (D) none of these

8. $135 \div 5 =$
   - (F) 71
   - (G) 17
   - (H) 27
   - (J) none of these

9. $490 \div 7 =$
   - (A) 70
   - (B) 60
   - (C) 50
   - (D) none of these

10. $880 \div 2 =$
   - (F) 401
   - (G) 440
   - (H) 400
   - (J) none of these

STOP

Mathematics

| 1.C |

Estimating
Number and Operations

DIRECTIONS: Choose the best answer.

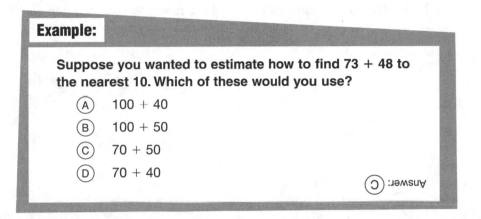

Example:

Suppose you wanted to estimate how to find 73 + 48 to the nearest 10. Which of these would you use?

- (A) 100 + 40
- (B) 100 + 50
- (C) 70 + 50
- (D) 70 + 40

Answer: (C)

1. Which of these is the best way to estimate the answer to this problem?

   28 − 19 = ▧

   - (A) 30 − 10 = ▧
   - (B) 20 − 10 = ▧
   - (C) 30 − 20 = ▧
   - (D) 10 − 10 = ▧

2. Which number sentence would you use to estimate 97 + 9 to the nearest 10?

   - (F) 90 + 5
   - (G) 100 + 10
   - (H) 90 + 10
   - (J) 100 + 5

3. Use estimation to find which of these is closest to 100.

   - (A) 59 + 57
   - (B) 49 + 40
   - (C) 39 + 58
   - (D) 91 + 18

4. A group of people brought their pets to a street fair. 33 people brought dogs, 18 people brought cats, and 11 people brought other kinds of pets. Which of these estimates is closest to the total number of people who brought pets?

   - (F) 50
   - (G) 60
   - (H) 70
   - (J) 80

5. Michael was at a card convention. At the first booth he bought 8 cards. He bought 6 cards at the next booth and 13 at the last booth. Which of these estimates is closest to the total number of cards Michael bought?

   - (A) 10
   - (B) 15
   - (C) 20
   - (D) 25

6. Use estimation to find which of these is closest to 80.

   - (F) 32 + 26
   - (G) 45 + 26
   - (H) 78 + 15
   - (J) 28 + 42

Mathematics

2.A

Extending Patterns
Algebra

DIRECTIONS: Choose the best answer.

1. **What number is missing from the sequence?**

3	6		12	15

- (A) 8
- (B) 9
- (C) 10
- (D) 11

2. **What number is missing from the sequence?**

11	22		44	55

- (F) 33
- (G) 23
- (H) 66
- (J) 42

3. **What number is missing from the sequence?**

6	12	18		30

- (A) 20
- (B) 24
- (C) 22
- (D) 26

4. **What number is missing from the sequence?**

29	33	37	41	

- (F) 43
- (G) 44
- (H) 45
- (J) 46

5. **Look at the pattern below. Which grouping is missing from the pattern?**

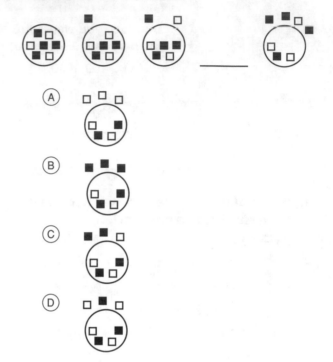

6. **Look at the pattern. Which shape below should come next in the pattern?**

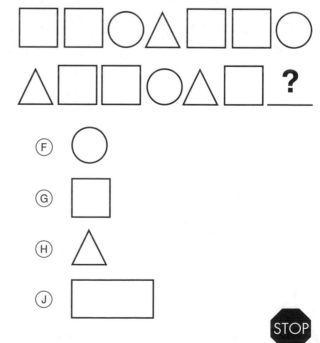

Mathematics

| 2.B |

Using Variables and Equations
Algebra

DIRECTIONS: Choose the best answer.

1. **What number makes this number sentence true?** $\blacksquare \times 4 = 8$
   - (A) 1
   - (B) 2
   - (C) 0
   - (D) 4

2. **What number makes this number sentence true?** $\blacksquare \times 3 = 9$
   - (F) 0
   - (G) 2
   - (H) 3
   - (J) 4

3. **What number makes this number sentence true?** $\blacksquare \div 2 = 7$
   - (A) 9
   - (B) 5
   - (C) 3
   - (D) 14

4. **What number makes this number sentence true?** $\blacksquare - 37 = 53$
   - (F) 100
   - (G) 110
   - (H) 90
   - (J) 89

5. **What number makes this number sentence true?** $\blacksquare \div 4 = 51$
   - (A) 204
   - (B) 240
   - (C) 47
   - (D) 55

DIRECTIONS: Choose the equation that best describes the text.

6. **Mrs. Tram's class lines up in 6 equal lines. There are 24 students in her class. How many students are in each line?**
   - (F) $6 \times 24 = \blacksquare$
   - (G) $24 \times \blacksquare = 6$
   - (H) $6 + \blacksquare = 24$
   - (J) $24 \div 6 = \blacksquare$

7. **The park ranger sees 8 rabbits running into the woods. How many legs does the park ranger see?**
   - (A) $8 + 4 = \blacksquare$
   - (B) $8 - 4 = \blacksquare$
   - (C) $8 \times 4 = \blacksquare$
   - (D) $8 \div 4 = \blacksquare$

8. **Stan's class is studying 11 different animals in science class. They have 7 animals left to study. How many animals have they studied already?**
   - (F) $\blacksquare + 11 = 7$
   - (G) $11 - 7 = \blacksquare$
   - (H) $11 + 7 = \blacksquare$
   - (J) $\blacksquare - 7 = 11$

9. **Beth bought an ice-cream cone for $1.25. She paid with a $5 bill. What is Beth's change?**
   - (A) $\$5.00 - \$1.25 = \blacksquare$
   - (B) $\$1.25 - \blacksquare = \$5.00$
   - (C) $\$1.25 + \$5.00 = \blacksquare$
   - (D) $\$1.25 \times \blacksquare = \$5.00$

Mathematics

2.C

Using Tables
Algebra

DIRECTIONS: The function machine uses rules to change numbers. Look for a pattern in the IN and OUT numbers in each table. Determine which function you need to use to get from each IN number to the OUT number beneath it. You will need to add, subtract, multiply, or divide. The same function and number is used for the entire table. Fill in the table. Then, write the rule for getting from the IN number to the OUT number.

Example:

IN	3	8	13	19
OUT	5	10		21

For this table, you must add 2 to each "in" number to find each "out" number. The missing number in this table is 15. The rule is: Add 2.

1.

IN	78	15	41	22	37		55
OUT	68	5	31			3	

Rule: _____

2.

IN	2	9	81	76	37		
OUT	11	18		85		34	51

Rule: _____

3.

IN	12	16	30	34	44		60
OUT	6	8			22	25	

Rule: _____

STOP

Mathematics

| 2.D |

Rates of Change
Algebra

DIRECTIONS: Study the pattern and answer the questions.

1. **Look for a pattern in the following shapes. Then, draw the fifth shape in this pattern in the space below.**

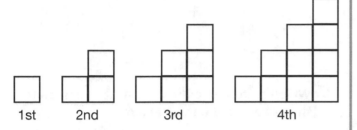

1st   2nd   3rd   4th

3. **Look at all the shapes in the pattern, including the ones you drew for questions 1 and 2. Then, fill in the table.**

Shape	Number of Tiles
1st	1
2nd	3
3rd	6
4th	10
5th	
6th	
7th	
8th	

4. **Explain how the pattern grows.**

_____

_____

_____

_____

_____

_____

2. **Now draw the sixth shape in this pattern in the space below.**

5. **If the pattern continues, how many tiles will be in the 9th shape?** _____

Mathematics

1.0–2.0

For pages 45–53

Mini-Test 1

Numbers and Operations; Algebra

DIRECTIONS: Choose the best answer.

1. **If you arranged these numbers from least to greatest, which would be last?**

   1,038 1,084 1,308 1,208 1,803

   - (A) 1,803
   - (B) 1,208
   - (C) 1,084
   - (D) 1,308

2. **How would you estimate 73 × 48 to the nearest 10?**

   - (F) 100 × 40
   - (G) 100 × 50
   - (H) 70 × 50
   - (J) 70 × 40

3. **How can you write 3,776 in expanded notation?**

   - (A) 3,000 + 700 + 70 + 6
   - (B) 3,000 + 700 + 76
   - (C) 3 + 7 + 7 + 6
   - (D) 3,000 + 776

4. **5 × ■ = 35; 35 ÷ ■ = 5**

   - (F) 6
   - (G) 5
   - (H) 7
   - (J) 35

5. **9 × 8 = ■**

   - (A) 72
   - (B) 63
   - (C) 64
   - (D) 81

6. **Which picture should come next to complete the pattern in the model below?**

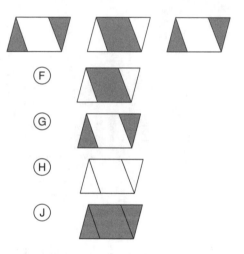

   - (F)
   - (G)
   - (H)
   - (J)

7. **Which series of numbers completes the function table?**

IN	12	14	16	18	20
OUT	15	17			

   - (A) 19, 22, 23
   - (B) 19, 21, 23
   - (C) 18, 21, 23
   - (D) 19, 21, 24

Mathematics

Matching Two- and Three-Dimensional Shapes
Geometry

DIRECTIONS: Match each three-dimensional shape with a corresponding two-dimensional shape by drawing a line. Some shapes will have more than one line.

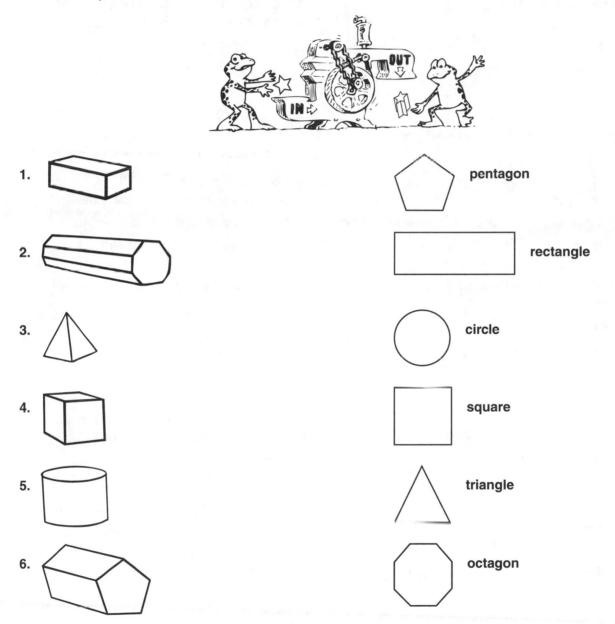

1.

2.

3.

4.

5.

6.

pentagon

rectangle

circle

square

triangle

octagon

7. **Name some objects in your classroom or house with the above shapes. For each object, identify the corresponding two-dimensional shape.**

_____

_____

_____

Mathematics

3.A

Identifying
Geometric Figures

Geometry

DIRECTIONS: Choose the best answer.

1. This shape is called a(n) _____ .

   (A) pentagon
   (B) hexagon
   (C) octagon
   (D) triangle

2. A polygon that has 6 sides and 6 angles is a(n) _____ .

   (F) pentagon
   (G) hexagon
   (H) octagon
   (J) trapezoid

3. Which polygon has more sides than a hexagon?

   (A) pentagon
   (B) triangle
   (C) octagon
   (D) square

4. How many sides does a quadrilateral have?

   (F) 3 sides
   (G) 4 sides
   (H) 5 sides
   (J) 6 sides

5. A polygon that has only one pair of parallel sides is a _____ .

   (A) parallelogram
   (B) quadrilateral
   (C) hexagon
   (D) trapezoid

6. A four-sided figure that has opposite sides that are parallel is called a _____ .

   (F) pentagon
   (G) parallelogram
   (H) triangle
   (J) hexagon

7. How is a square different from a rectangle?

   (A) A square has four equal sides.
   (B) A square has two equal sides.
   (C) A square has right angles.
   (D) A square has parallel sides.

8. A shape with 5 sides is known as what?

   (F) a rectangle
   (G) a hexagon
   (H) a pentagon
   (J) an octagon

9. If you were to draw a figure with no sides and no angles, what would it look like?

   (A)
   (B)
   (C)
   (D)

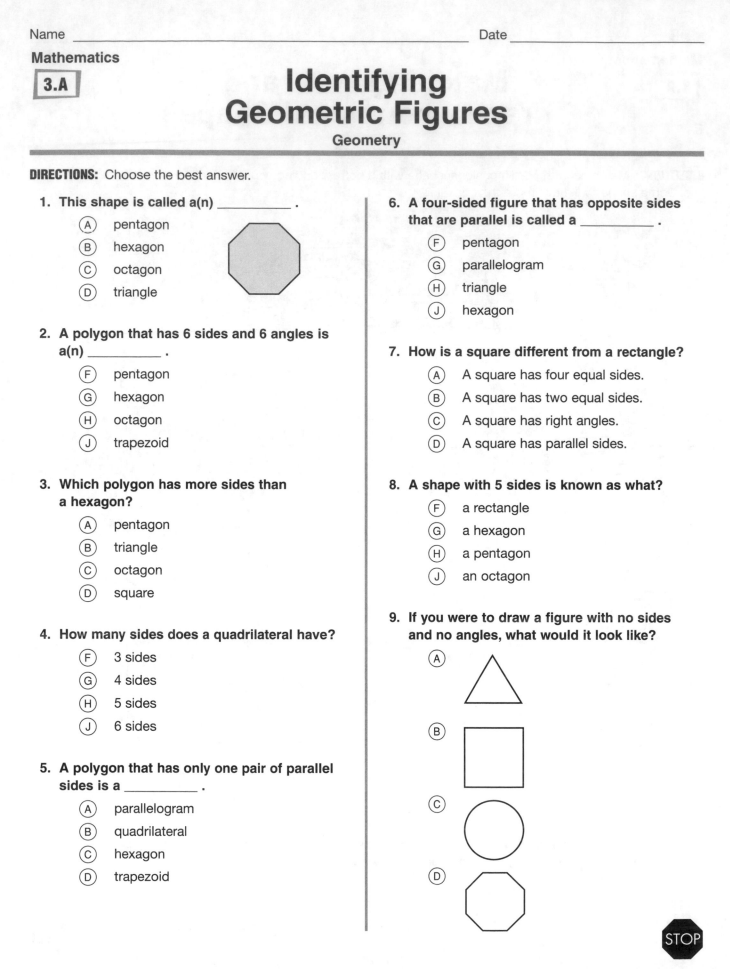

Name _____ Date _____

Using Coordinates
Geometry

DIRECTIONS: On the grid below, plot the points that are given at the bottom of this page. Label each point with its corresponding letter. Point **L,** the library, has been plotted for you at (4, 5). Remember, the first number represents the horizontal axis, known as the *x-axis,* and the second number represents the vertical axis, known as the *y-axis.*

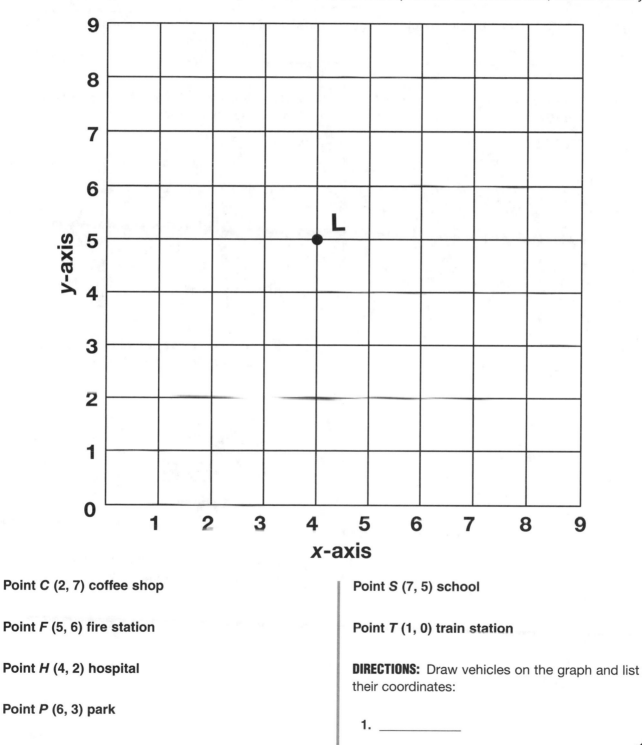

Point C (2, 7) coffee shop

Point F (5, 6) fire station

Point H (4, 2) hospital

Point P (6, 3) park

Point S (7, 5) school

Point T (1, 0) train station

DIRECTIONS: Draw vehicles on the graph and list their coordinates:

1. _____

2. _____

Symmetry and Reflection
Geometry

DIRECTIONS: Read each question. Choose the best answer.

Clue Remember that if you fold the figure on the line of symmetry, the two halves match up perfectly.

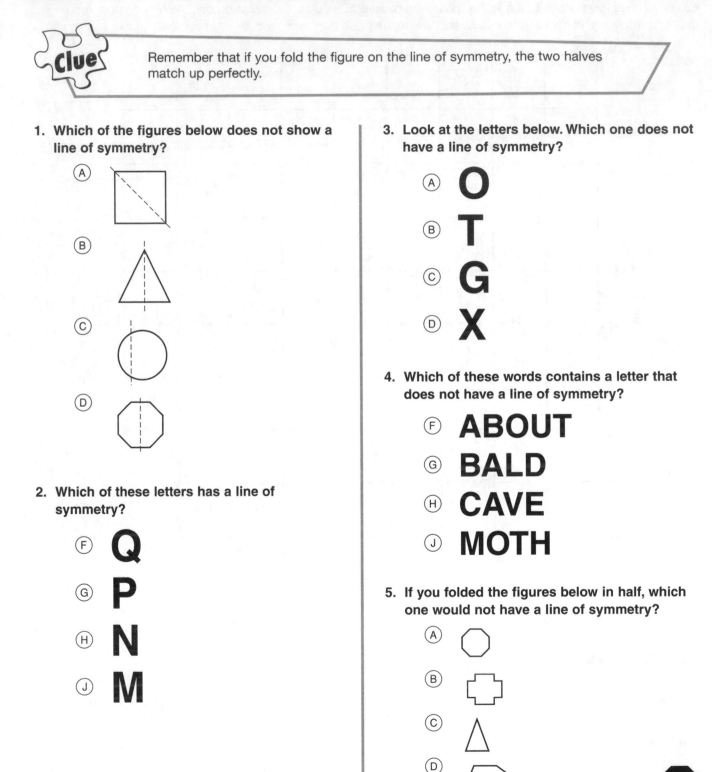

1. Which of the figures below does not show a line of symmetry?

2. Which of these letters has a line of symmetry?

3. Look at the letters below. Which one does not have a line of symmetry?
   - A O
   - B T
   - C G
   - D X

4. Which of these words contains a letter that does not have a line of symmetry?
   - F ABOUT
   - G BALD
   - H CAVE
   - J MOTH

5. If you folded the figures below in half, which one would not have a line of symmetry?

Mathematics

| 3.C |

Reflection and Rotation
Geometry

DIRECTIONS: For the drawings below, write *reflection* or *rotation* to describe how the figure was moved.

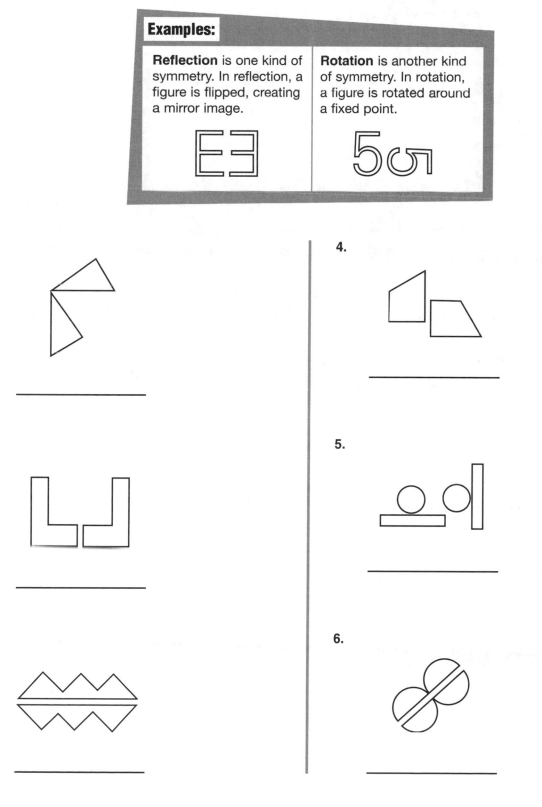

Examples:

Reflection is one kind of symmetry. In reflection, a figure is flipped, creating a mirror image.

Rotation is another kind of symmetry. In rotation, a figure is rotated around a fixed point.

1.

_____

2.

_____

3.

_____

4.

_____

5.

_____

6.

_____

Mathematics

3.D

Drawing
Three-Dimensional Objects
Geometry

Example:

A basketball is shaped like a _____.

- Ⓐ pyramid
- Ⓑ circle
- Ⓒ sphere
- Ⓓ rectangle

Answer: C.

Clue   Imagine what each object looks like before choosing your answer.

DIRECTIONS: Choose the best answer for numbers 1–3.

1. A cereal box is shaped like a _____.

- Ⓐ pyramid
- Ⓑ sphere
- Ⓒ rectangular prism
- Ⓓ cone

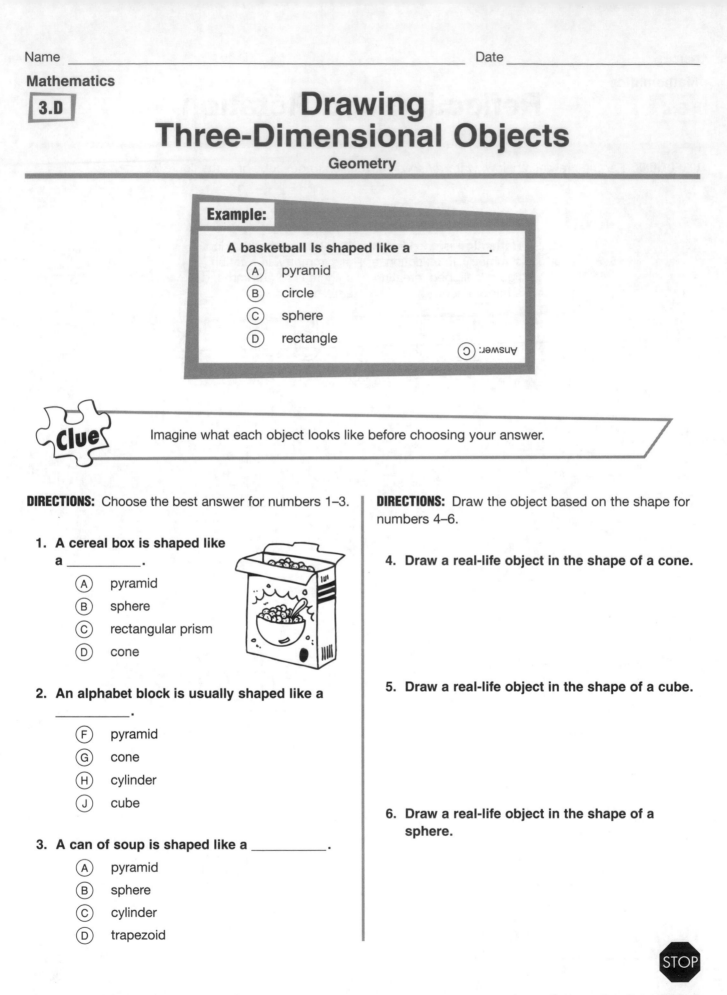

2. An alphabet block is usually shaped like a _____.

- Ⓕ pyramid
- Ⓖ cone
- Ⓗ cylinder
- Ⓙ cube

3. A can of soup is shaped like a _____.

- Ⓐ pyramid
- Ⓑ sphere
- Ⓒ cylinder
- Ⓓ trapezoid

DIRECTIONS: Draw the object based on the shape for numbers 4–6.

4. Draw a real-life object in the shape of a cone.

5. Draw a real-life object in the shape of a cube.

6. Draw a real-life object in the shape of a sphere.

STOP

Mathematics

4.A

Measuring Objects
Measurement

DIRECTIONS: Choose the best answer.

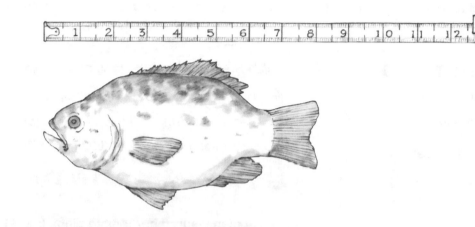

1. **How many inches long is the fish?**

   (A) 5 inches

   (B) 6 inches

   (C) 8 inches

   (D) 12 inches

2. **Look at the paper clip and the pencils. Which pencil is about three inches longer than the paper clip?**

   (F)

   (G)

   (H)

   (J)

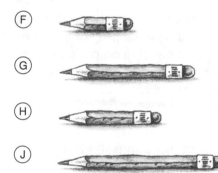

3. **Angela wants to measure a piece of wood. Which of these should she use?**

   (A)   (B)   (C)   (D)

STOP

Mathematics

4.A

Comparing Units of Length

Measurement

DIRECTIONS: Fill in the blanks with the equivalent measurement. Below is a chart of customary length conversions. Use the chart to help you answer the questions.

> 1 foot = 12 inches
>
> 1 yard = 3 feet
>
> 1 mile = 5,280 feet

1. 7 yards = _____ feet

2. 24 inches = _____ feet

3. 6 feet = _____ yard(s)

4. 10 miles = _____ feet

5. 60 inches = _____ feet

6. 30 feet = _____ yard(s)

7. 5 feet + 2 inches = _____ inches

8. 3 feet = _____ inches

DIRECTIONS: The metric measuring system is based on multiples of 10. Below is a chart of metric length conversions. Use the chart to help you answer the questions.

> 1 centimeter (cm) = 10 millimeters (mm)
>
> 1 meter (m) = 100 centimeters (cm)
>
> 1 kilometer (km) = 1,000 meters (m)

9. Jodi measured her tomato plant. It is 34 centimeters. How many millimeters is this? _____

10. Meg has a plastic case that is 4 centimeters long. She found a shell that is 34 millimeters long. Will it fit in her case? _____

11. Kifa jumped 3 meters. How many centimeters is this? _____

12. Jordan's desk is 1 meter by 1 meter. He would like to put his science project inside his desk. The science project is on poster board that is 95 centimeters by 110 centimeters. Will it fit inside his desk without sticking out? _____

13. Amar's room measures 10 meters by 12 meters. What is the room's measurement in centimeters? _____

Mathematics

4.B

Estimating Measurement
Measurement

DIRECTIONS: Choose the best answer.

1. Toby left his house for school at 7:33 A.M. He arrived to school at 7:50 A.M. About how many minutes did it take Toby to get to school?

(A) 15 minutes

(B) 25 minutes

(C) 30 minutes

(D) 10 minutes

2. Lillian rode her bicycle to the supermarket to buy some items for her mother. Here is the change she was given when she bought one of the items below with a five-dollar bill. Which item did she buy?

(F)
Detergent 3.50

(G)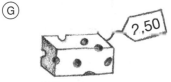
?.50

(H)
IceCream 2.95

(J)
Coffee 3.65

3. Which of these is most likely measured in feet?

(A) the distance around a room

(B) the weight of a large box

(C) the distance to the moon

(D) the amount of water in a pool

4. Lukas, Maria, and Keith decided to weigh themselves this morning. Lukas weighs 83 pounds, Maria weighs 79 pounds, and Keith weighs 98 pounds. About how much do they weigh altogether?

(F) 230 pounds

(G) 260 pounds

(H) 240 pounds

(J) 270 pounds

5. The zoo can't let the animals outside unless the temperature is higher than 50° by 10 A.M. The temperature at 10 A.M. on Monday was 42°. On Tuesday, the temperature was 9° warmer. Was it warm enough to let the animals out on Tuesday?

(A) yes

(B) no

DIRECTIONS: For each of the following figures, estimate the area of the shaded part. Choose the number that is most likely the area (in square units).

6. (F) 3
   (G) 5
   (H) 9
   (J) 2

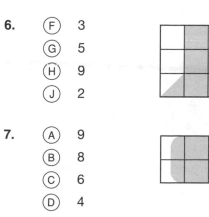

7. (A) 9
   (B) 8
   (C) 6
   (D) 4

STOP

Mathematics

4.B

Determining
Area and Perimeter

Measurement

DIRECTIONS: Choose the best answer.

Clue   The **perimeter** is the distance around the edge of a shape. The **area** is the amount of space occupied by a shape.

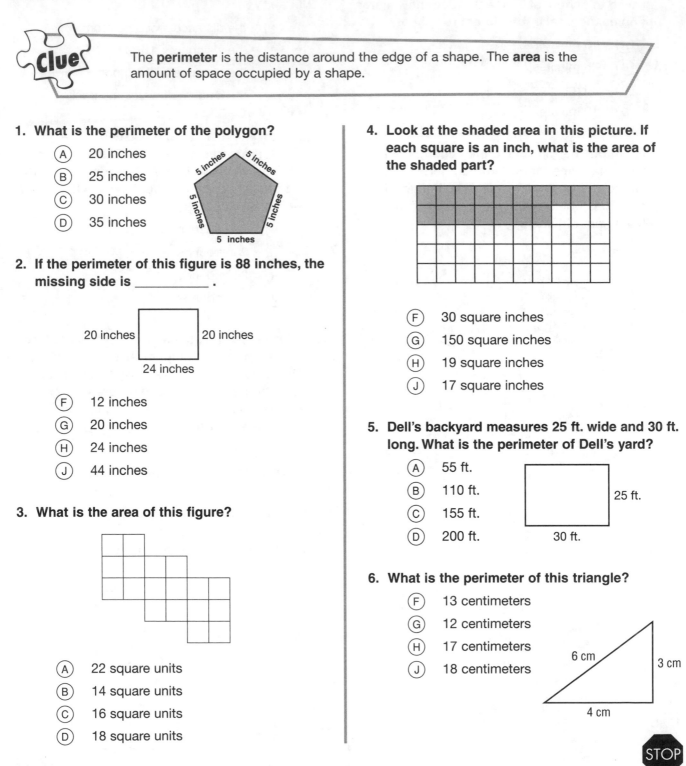

1. **What is the perimeter of the polygon?**

    Ⓐ   20 inches
    Ⓑ   25 inches
    Ⓒ   30 inches
    Ⓓ   35 inches

    5 inches   5 inches
    5 inches   5 inches
        5 inches
        5 inches

2. **If the perimeter of this figure is 88 inches, the missing side is _____ .**

    20 inches [   ] 20 inches
        24 inches

    Ⓕ   12 inches
    Ⓖ   20 inches
    Ⓗ   24 inches
    Ⓙ   44 inches

3. **What is the area of this figure?**

    Ⓐ   22 square units
    Ⓑ   14 square units
    Ⓒ   16 square units
    Ⓓ   18 square units

4. **Look at the shaded area in this picture. If each square is an inch, what is the area of the shaded part?**

    Ⓕ   30 square inches
    Ⓖ   150 square inches
    Ⓗ   19 square inches
    Ⓙ   17 square inches

5. **Dell's backyard measures 25 ft. wide and 30 ft. long. What is the perimeter of Dell's yard?**

    Ⓐ   55 ft.
    Ⓑ   110 ft.
    Ⓒ   155 ft.
    Ⓓ   200 ft.

    25 ft.
        30 ft.

6. **What is the perimeter of this triangle?**

    Ⓕ   13 centimeters
    Ⓖ   12 centimeters
    Ⓗ   17 centimeters
    Ⓙ   18 centimeters

    6 cm   3 cm
        4 cm

STOP

Mathematics

| 3.0–4.0 |
For pages 55–64

Mini-Test 2

Geometry; Measurement

DIRECTIONS: Choose the best answer.

1. This shape is called a(n) _____ .
   - (A) circle
   - (B) pentagon
   - (C) octagon
   - (D) hexagon

2. Which polygon has fewer sides than a square?
   - (F) pentagon
   - (G) triangle
   - (H) octagon
   - (J) square

3. What three solid objects have been used to make this object?

   - (A) sphere, cylinder, rectangular prism
   - (B) cube, cylinder, pyramid
   - (C) pyramid, cylinder, square
   - (D) cone, cylinder, cube

4. Which of these objects is shaped like a cube?
   - (F)
   - (H)
   - (G)
   - (J)

5. Which letter has a line of symmetry?
   - (A) **J**
   - (B) **S**
   - (C) **M**
   - (D) **Q**

6. Look at the shaded area in this square. If each square is an inch, what is the area of the shaded part?
   - (F) 16 square inches
   - (G) 15 square inches
   - (H) 12 square inches
   - (J) 10 square inches

7. How many inches are in two feet?
   - (A) 18 inches
   - (B) 36 inches
   - (C) 24 inches
   - (D) 12 inches

8. Elana wants to put a fence around her flower garden. How many feet of fencing will she need?

   4 ft.
   3 ft.
   5 ft.
   10 ft.

   - (F) 22 ft.
   - (G) 50 ft.
   - (H) 62 ft.
   - (J) 33 ft.

STOP

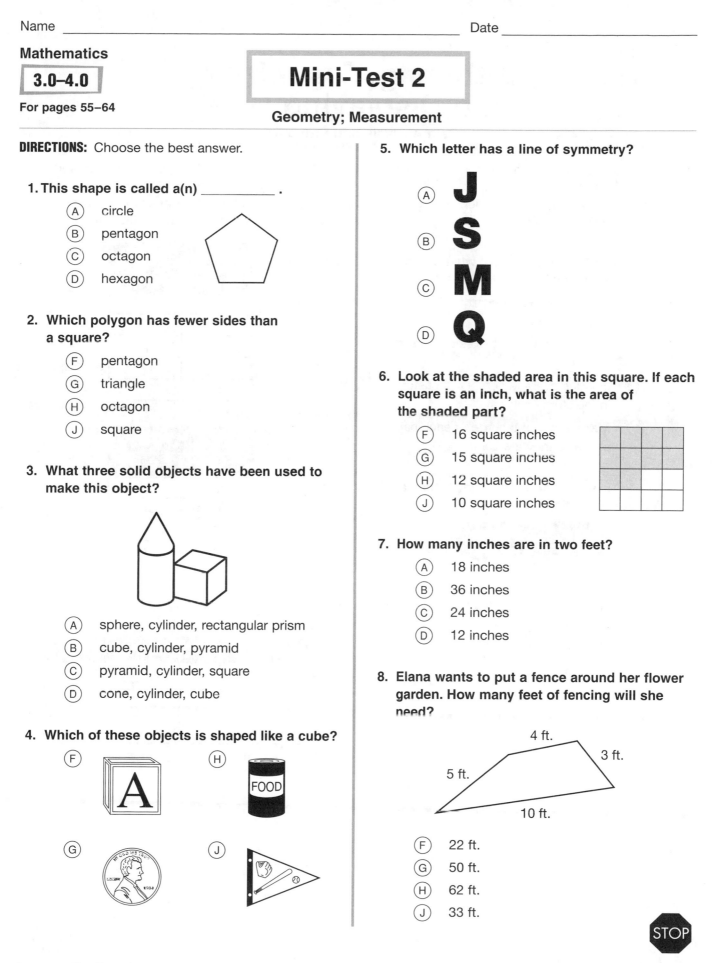

Mathematics

| 5.A/5.B/5.C |

Gathering, Organizing, and Displaying Data

Data Analysis and Probability

DIRECTIONS: Tia was helping out in her dad's shoe store. She thinks that the store sells more of some sizes than others. Answer the questions below about how Tia can find out if this is true.

1. **What could Tia do to find out what size shoes are sold each day?**

   Ⓐ Ask everyone in the store what size shoe they wear.

   Ⓑ Count all the shoe boxes at the end of every day.

   Ⓒ Find the average number of customers in the store each day.

   Ⓓ Make a tally of the size of each pair of shoes as they are sold.

2. **This is Tia's tally for the first day. What can Tia find out from this tally?**

Tally for 1st Day	
Size	Tally
5	//
6	////
7	///
8	///
9	/

   Ⓕ the color of the shoes sold

   Ⓖ how many pairs of shoes each customer bought

   Ⓗ the size of each pair of shoes sold

   Ⓙ how many boxes of shoes the store owns

3. **These are Tia's tallies for the second and third days. Fill in the table to show the total number of shoes sold in each size for all three days. The first day's tallies are in**

Tally for 2nd Day	
Size	Tally
5	/
6	////
7	//
8	/
9	

Tally for 3rd Day	
Size	Tally
5	//
6	ℍℍ
7	///
8	//
9	/

Shoe Size	Total Pairs Sold
5	
6	
7	
8	
9	

GO

Clue

The **median** is the number in the middle when a group of numbers is arranged in order from least to greatest.

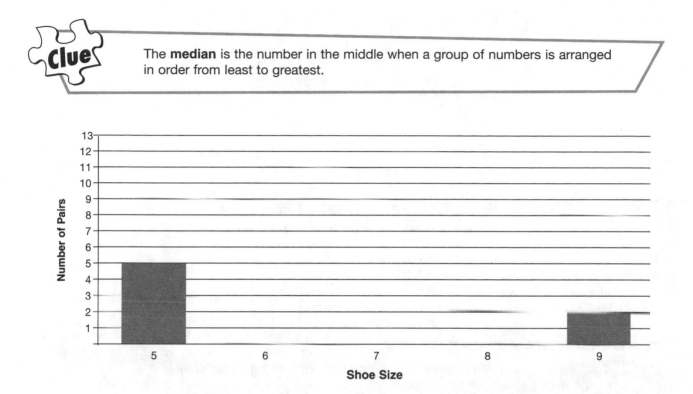

4. **Add the bars missing from the graph to show the number of shoes sold in each size.**

5. **What does Tia know from all of the information she has gathered?**

   - (A) More size 5 shoes were sold.
   - (B) More size 6 shoes were sold.
   - (C) More size 7 shoes were sold.
   - (D) More size 8 shoes were sold.

6. **Was Tia correct in thinking the store sells more of some sizes than others?**

   - (F) yes
   - (G) no

7. **Look at the table you completed in question 3. Arrange the numbers for the total pairs sold in order from the least to the greatest. What is the median for the total pairs of shoes that were sold?**

   - (A) 5
   - (B) 6
   - (C) 8
   - (D) 12

8. **What can Tia predict now?**

   - (F) The black shoes are the most popular.
   - (G) More customers wear size 6 than other sizes.
   - (H) More customers wear size 9 than other sizes.
   - (J) none of these

Mathematics

5.D

Determining Likelihood and Probability

Data Analysis and Probability

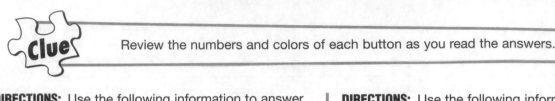

Clue Review the numbers and colors of each button as you read the answers.

DIRECTIONS: Use the following information to answer questions 1–4.

Melanie put 3 yellow buttons, 6 red buttons, 2 blue buttons, and 1 green button in a bag. Mikel draws one button out of the bag each time. Answer the questions below.

1. **What is the chance that Mikel will pull out a yellow button?**

   Ⓐ 3 out of 12
   Ⓑ 4 out of 12
   Ⓒ 1 out of 12
   Ⓓ 6 out of 12

2. **What is the chance that Mikel will pull out a blue button?**

   Ⓕ 1 out of 12
   Ⓖ 4 out of 12
   Ⓗ 5 out of 12
   Ⓙ 2 out of 12

3. **Which color is Mikel most likely to pull out?**

   Ⓐ yellow
   Ⓑ blue
   Ⓒ red
   Ⓓ green

4. **Which color is Mikel least likely to pull out?**

   Ⓕ yellow
   Ⓖ blue
   Ⓗ red
   Ⓙ green

DIRECTIONS: Use the following information for questions 5–7.

In a grocery bag, there are 6 cans of tomato sauce, 4 cans of beans, and 9 cans of olives. All the cans are the same size.

5. **If you reached into the bag without looking and picked out a can, what is the probability of picking a can of olives?**

   Ⓐ $\frac{1}{19}$
   Ⓑ $\frac{4}{19}$
   Ⓒ $\frac{6}{19}$
   Ⓓ $\frac{9}{19}$

6. **What is the probability of picking a can of beans?**

   Ⓕ $\frac{1}{19}$
   Ⓖ $\frac{4}{19}$
   Ⓗ $\frac{6}{19}$
   Ⓙ $\frac{9}{19}$

7. **What is the probability of picking a can of tomato sauce?**

   Ⓐ $\frac{1}{19}$
   Ⓑ $\frac{4}{19}$
   Ⓒ $\frac{6}{19}$
   Ⓓ $\frac{9}{19}$

Mathematics

6.A

Solving Problems
Process

DIRECTIONS: Choose the best answer.

1. The music store had 757 customers last month and 662 customers this month. How many customers did the store have altogether in those two months?

   (A) 1,409 customers

   (B) 1,419 customers

   (C) 1,429 customers

   (D) 1,439 customers

2. Janna has invited 5 girls and 3 boys to her birthday party. She plans to give each of her guests two balloons and keep one for herself. How many balloons will she need in all?

   (F) 17 balloons

   (G) 9 balloons

   (H) 8 balloons

   (J) 18 balloons

3. Cody played in 3 basketball games. In the first game, he scored 17 points. In the second game, he scored 22 points. In the third game, he scored twice as many points as in his first game. How many points did he score in the third game?

   (A) 44 points

   (B) 36 points

   (C) 34 points

   (D) 42 points

4. Amir has $3.00 to buy lunch. He chooses a sandwich that costs $1.50 and an orange that costs $0.45. How much money does he have left?

   (F) $0.05

   (G) $1.05

   (H) $1.15

   (J) $1.60

5. The trip from Homeville to Lincoln usually takes 25 minutes by car. While making the trip, a driver spent 12 minutes getting gas and 5 minutes waiting for a road crew. How long did it take the driver to make the trip?

   (A) 32 minutes

   (B) 37 minutes

   (C) 48 minutes

   (D) 42 minutes

6. The price of bread was $1.29, but it increased by 8 cents. What was the new price of the bread?

   (F) $1.21

   (G) $1.36

   (H) $1.37

   (J) $1.39

7. Arnell wants to buy 3 books. Each book costs $3.95. How much will it cost to pay for all the books?

   (A) $11.85

   (B) $12.55

   (C) $7.90

   (D) $9.50

8. Michael has 4 quarters and 2 dimes for bus fare. If the bus ride costs $0.75, how much money will he have left?

   (F) $0.25

   (G) $0.35

   (H) $0.45

   (J) $0.50

Evaluating Mathematical Arguments

Process

DIRECTIONS: Choose the best answer.

1. Michael has five pieces of candy. How many pieces would he have if he adds five additional pieces each minute for three minutes?

   (A) 15

   (B) 20

   (C) 25

   (D) none of these

2. Which number sentence shows how to verify the answer to question 1?

   (F) $5 + 10 = 15$

   (G) $5 \times 3 + 5 = 20$

   (H) $5 \times 5 = 25$

   (J) none of these

3. Tai carried four boxes of tiles into the kitchen. Each box held 12 tiles. How would you best determine the total number of tiles he carried into the kitchen?

   (A) multiply

   (B) subtract

   (C) divide

   (D) none of these

4. Which number sentence proves the total number of tiles Tai carried into the kitchen?

   (F) $4 \times 12 = 48$

   (G) $12 - 4 = 8$

   (H) $48 \div 8 = 6$

   (J) none of these

5. There are 762 CD titles listed in the computer. Macy enters 292 new titles into the computer. To find the total number of CD titles listed now, which operation would you use?

   (A) addition

   (B) subtraction

   (C) multiplication

   (D) division

6. The store sells 5 cans of peas for $1.25. Which operation helps you find out how much each can costs?

   (F) addition

   (G) subtraction

   (H) multiplication

   (J) division

7. This map shows Janelle's yard. She came in through the gate and walked three yards in one direction, then turned and went two yards in a different direction. She ended up closest to the steps. In which directions can you predict that she traveled?

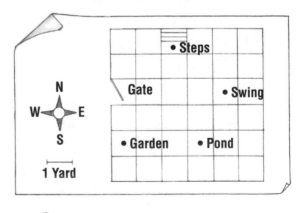

   (A) east and north

   (B) south and east

   (C) west and south

   (D) north and west

Mathematics

Using Mathematical Language

Process

DIRECTIONS: Choose the best answer.

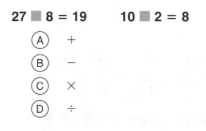 When you are not sure of an answer, make your best guess and move on to the next problem.

1. **Which operation sign belongs in both boxes?**

   27 ■ 8 = 19   10 ■ 2 = 8

   Ⓐ +
   Ⓑ −
   Ⓒ ×
   Ⓓ ÷

2. **You have a bag of candy to share with your class. There are 25 students in your class. You want each student to get 7 pieces. What operation will you need to use to figure out how many candies you need?**

   Ⓕ addition
   Ⓖ subtraction
   Ⓗ multiplication
   Ⓙ division

3. **Tad wants to find the weight of a box of cereal. What unit of measurement will he probably find on the side of the box?**

   Ⓐ millimeters
   Ⓑ pounds
   Ⓒ hectoliters
   Ⓓ ounces

4. **Which of these numbers shows 587 rounded to the nearest hundred?**

   Ⓕ 580
   Ⓖ 600
   Ⓗ 690
   Ⓙ 500

5. **Which of these numbers has a 1 in the tens place and a 7 in the ones place?**

   Ⓐ 710
   Ⓑ 701
   Ⓒ 517
   Ⓓ 471

6. **What sign correctly completes the number sentence?**

   24 ■ 6 = 4

   Ⓕ ÷
   Ⓖ −
   Ⓗ +
   Ⓙ ×

7. **Which decimal is equal to $\frac{1}{4}$?**

   Ⓐ 0.25
   Ⓑ 0.025
   Ⓒ 0.75
   Ⓓ 0.033

8. **Which amount is the same as 25 cents?**

   Ⓕ $\frac{1}{4}$ dollar
   Ⓖ $\frac{1}{2}$ dollar
   Ⓗ $\frac{2}{3}$ dollar
   Ⓙ $\frac{3}{4}$ dollar

STOP

Name _____   Date _____

Connecting and Representing Mathematical Ideas

Process

DIRECTIONS: The third-grade students at Zinser Elementary were asked to do reports on one of the following five birds: hummingbird, hawk, owl, blue jay, or California condor. Use the graph below to answer questions 1–3.

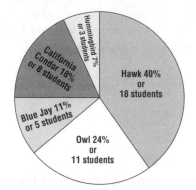

1. **Which of the following lists the birds from least to most favorite?**

   Ⓐ hawk, owl, California condor, blue jay, hummingbird

   Ⓑ blue jay, hummingbird, California condor, owl, hawk

   Ⓒ hummingbird, blue jay, California condor, owl, hawk

   Ⓓ California condor, hawk, owl, blue jay, hummingbird

2. **Which two kinds of birds combined below got more than 50 percent of the vote?**

   Ⓕ hawk and owl

   Ⓖ hummingbird and California condor

   Ⓗ hummingbird and blue jay

   Ⓙ hawk and hummingbird

3. **What percent of the vote do the hummingbird, California condor, and blue jay make up together?**

   Ⓐ 40%

   Ⓑ 25%

   Ⓒ 30%

   Ⓓ 36%

DIRECTIONS: Choose the best answer.

4. **Sarah just read that her town has the highest population in the county. Based on the chart below, in which city does Sarah live?**

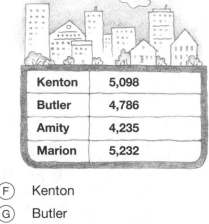

Kenton	5,098
Butler	4,786
Amity	4,235
Marion	5,232

   Ⓕ Kenton

   Ⓖ Butler

   Ⓗ Amity

   Ⓙ Marion

DIRECTIONS: Solve the following problem using paper and pencil. Write directions or show the steps for solving the problem in the space provided.

5. **Taina had a rectangle made out of paper. She drew a line down the middle of the rectangle. Then she drew a line across the middle of the rectangle. She had drawn 4 shapes. What shapes did she draw?**

   Ⓐ square

   Ⓑ rhombus

   Ⓒ triangle

   Ⓓ rectangle

Mathematics

5.0–6.0

For pages 66–72

Mini-Test 3

Data Analysis and Probability; Process

DIRECTIONS: Choose the best answer.

1. Ryan flipped a coin. What are the chances that it will come up tails?

   (A) 0

   (B) 1 in 1

   (C) 1 in 2

   (D) 2 in 2

2. A number cube is rolled. What is the probability of rolling a two?

   (F) $\frac{1}{2}$

   (G) $\frac{1}{4}$

   (H) $\frac{1}{6}$

   (J) $\frac{1}{8}$

3. There were 485 balloons decorating the gymnasium for a party. There were 97 students at the party. Each student brought home an equal number of balloons after the party. How many balloons did each student bring home?

   (A) 3 balloons

   (B) 4 balloons

   (C) 5 balloons

   (D) 6 balloons

4. If you burn 318 calories in 60 minutes of playing tennis, how many calories would you burn in 30 minutes?

   (F) 159 calories

   (G) 636 calories

   (H) 258 calories

   (J) 288 calories

DIRECTIONS: Study the graph. Use the information to answer questions 5–7.

Top Countries Generating Hydroelectric Power

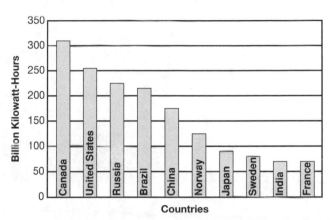

5. Which country below produces the least amount of hydroelectricity?

   (A) Brazil

   (B) China

   (C) India

   (D) Canada

6. Which country produces more hydroelectricity than Brazil and less than the United States?

   (F) Russia

   (G) China

   (H) Canada

   (J) Brazil

7. In which class would a graph like this most likely be used?

   (A) geography

   (B) music

   (C) English

   (D) gym

STOP

How Am I Doing?

Mini-Test 1 Page 54 **Number Correct**	**7** answers correct	**Great Job!** Move on to the section test on page 75.
	4–6 answers correct	**You're almost there!** But you still need a little practice. Review practice pages 45–53 before moving on to the section test on page 75.
	0–3 answers correct	**Oops!** Time to review what you have learned and try again. Review the practice section on pages 45–53. Then, retake the test on page 54. Now, move on to the section test on page 75.
Mini-Test 2 Page 65 **Number Correct**	**8** answers correct	**Awesome!** Move on to the section test on page 75.
	4–7 answers correct	**You're almost there!** But you still need a little practice. Review practice pages 55–64 before moving on to the section test on page 75.
	0–3 answers correct	**Oops!** Time to review what you have learned and try again. Review the practice section on pages 55–64. Then, retake the test on page 65. Now, move on to the section test on page 75.
Mini-Test 3 Page 73 **Number Correct**	**7** answers correct	**Great Job!** Move on to the section test on page 75.
	5–6 answers correct	**You're almost there!** But you still need a little practice. Review practice pages 66–72 before moving on to the section test on page 75.
	0–4 answers correct	**Oops!** Time to review what you have learned and try again. Review the practice section on pages 66–72. Then, retake the test on page 73. Now, move on to the section test on page 75.

Final Mathematics Test
for pages 45–73

DIRECTIONS: Choose the best answer.

1. **Which of these numbers is eight thousand, six hundred twenty-two?**

   (A) 8,622

   (B) 8,602

   (C) 862

   (D) 88,622

2. **If you arranged these numbers from least to greatest, which would be first?**

   3,090   3,990   3,190   3,009   3,099

   (F) 3,090

   (G) 3,099

   (H) 3,009

   (J) 3,190

3. **How can you write 26,345 in expanded notation?**

   (A) $26 + 34 + 5$

   (B) $2,600 + 3,400 + 5$

   (C) $26,000 + 6,000 + 300 + 45 + 1$

   (D) $20,000 + 6,000 + 300 + 40 + 5$

4. $11 \times \blacksquare = 33$

   (F) 1

   (G) 2

   (H) 3

   (J) none of these

5. $48 \div 6 =$

   (A) 8

   (B) 7

   (C) 9

   (D) none of these

6. **What is the next number after 3, 6, 9, 12?**

   (F) 13

   (G) 11

   (H) 15

   (J) 14

7. **Steph ran 2 miles each day for a week. Which number sentence describes how far she ran?**

   (A) $2 \times 4 = \blacksquare$

   (B) $7 \times 4 = \blacksquare$

   (C) $2 \times 7 = \blacksquare$

   (D) $2 \times 2 = \blacksquare$

DIRECTIONS: The points **M, N,** and **O** represent the houses of three friends—Matt, Nate, and Onan. Each square in the grid represents a square mile. The heavy black lines on the grid represent roads. Use the following grid to answer questions 8 and 9.

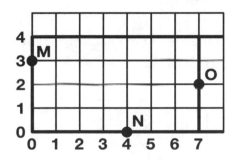

8. **What is the location of Matt's house?**

   (F) (1, 1)

   (G) (0, 3)

   (H) (4, 0)

   (J) (7, 2)

9. **What Is the location of Nate's house?**

   (A) (1, 1)

   (B) (0, 3)

   (C) (4, 0)

   (D) (7, 2)

GO

DIRECTIONS: Choose the best answer.

10. **Which letter has a line of symmetry?**

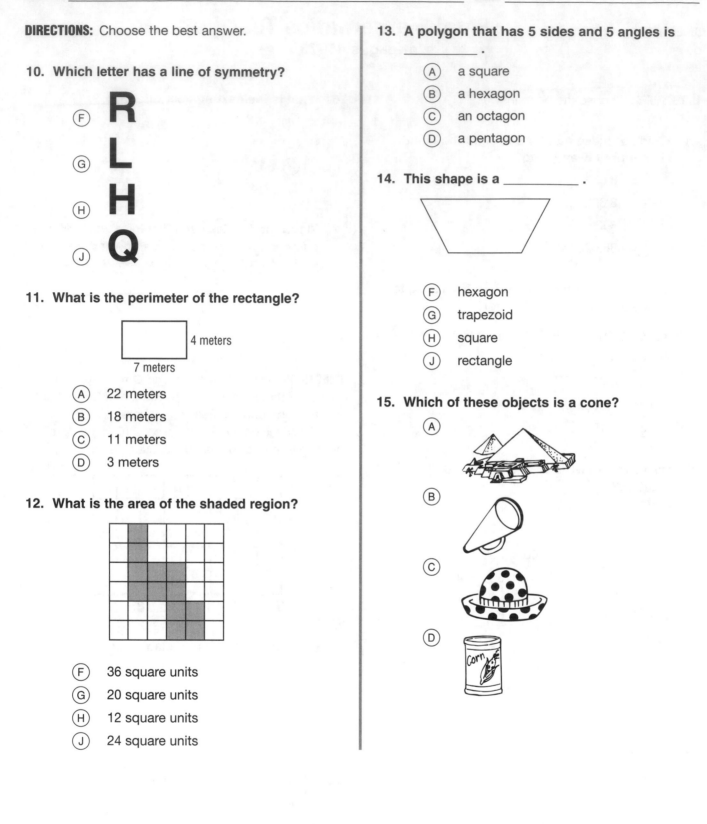

(F) R

(G) L

(H) H

(J) Q

11. **What is the perimeter of the rectangle?**

4 meters

7 meters

(A) 22 meters

(B) 18 meters

(C) 11 meters

(D) 3 meters

12. **What is the area of the shaded region?**

(F) 36 square units

(G) 20 square units

(H) 12 square units

(J) 24 square units

13. **A polygon that has 5 sides and 5 angles is _____ .**

(A) a square

(B) a hexagon

(C) an octagon

(D) a pentagon

14. **This shape is a _____ .**

(F) hexagon

(G) trapezoid

(H) square

(J) rectangle

15. **Which of these objects is a cone?**

(A)

(B)

(C)

(D)

Name _____   Date _____

DIRECTIONS: Use the bar graph below to answer questions 16–18. The information in the graph is about Mrs. Coleson's class and their favorite cafeteria lunch. All the students are represented in the graph.

Students' Favorite Cafeteria Lunches

A bar graph titled "Students' Favorite Cafeteria Lunches." The vertical axis is labeled "Number of Students" ranging from 0 to 10. The horizontal axis is labeled "Types of Lunches" with the categories: hamburger with fries (10), salad with bread (8), chicken patty (4), taco with chips (6), spaghetti (8).

Types of Lunches

16. Which lunch did the students like the most?
- (F) hamburger with fries
- (G) spaghetti
- (H) chicken patty
- (J) taco with chips

17. Which lunches did the same number of students like?
- (A) chicken patty and spaghetti
- (B) hamburger with fries and spaghetti
- (C) taco with chips and chicken patty
- (D) salad with bread and spaghetti

18. How many students chose taco with chips as their favorite lunch?
- (F) 5
- (G) 6
- (H) 3
- (J) 4

DIRECTIONS: Brad put 4 green jelly beans, 5 red jelly beans, 2 yellow jelly beans, and 1 purple jelly bean in a jar. His sister closed her eyes and pulled out one at a time.

19. What is the chance that his sister will pull out a yellow jelly bean?
- (A) 2 out of 12
- (B) 2 out of 2
- (C) 3 out of 8
- (D) 2 out of 10

20. Which color will his sister most likely pull out?
- (F) green
- (G) red
- (H) yellow
- (J) purple

21. Which color will his sister least likely pull out?
- (A) green
- (B) red
- (C) yellow
- (D) purple

DIRECTIONS: Choose the best answer.

22. A plane has 124 passengers, 3 pilots, and 9 flight attendants. What is the total number of people on the plane?
- (F) 136 people
- (G) 135 people
- (H) 133 people
- (J) 112 people

23. A babysitter works for 4 hours and earns $20. Which number sentence shows how to find the amount of money the babysitter earns in one hour?
- (A) $4 \times \$20 = \blacksquare$
- (B) $\$5 + \blacksquare = \$20$
- (C) $\$20 \div \$4 = \blacksquare$

STOP

Name _____   Date _____

Final Mathematics Test
Answer Sheet

1 (A) (B) (C) (D)
2 (F) (G) (H) (J)
3 (A) (B) (C) (D)
4 (F) (G) (H) (J)
5 (A) (B) (C) (D)
6 (F) (G) (H) (J)
7 (A) (B) (C) (D)
8 (F) (G) (H) (J)
9 (A) (B) (C) (D)
10 (F) (G) (H) (J)

11 (A) (B) (C) (D)
12 (F) (G) (H) (J)
13 (A) (B) (C) (D)
14 (F) (G) (H) (J)
15 (A) (B) (C) (D)
16 (F) (G) (H) (J)
17 (A) (B) (C) (D)
18 (F) (G) (H) (J)
19 (A) (B) (C) (D)
20 (F) (G) (H) (J)

21 (A) (B) (C) (D)
22 (F) (G) (H) (J)
23 (A) (B) (C) (D)

Social Studies Standards

Standard 1—Culture *(See pages 80–81.)*
Social studies programs should include experiences that provide for the study of culture and cultural diversity.

Standard 2—Time, Continuity, and Change *(See pages 82–83.)*
Social studies programs should include experiences that provide for the study of the way human beings view themselves in and over time.

Standard 3—People, Places, and Environments *(See pages 84–86.)*
Social studies programs should include experiences that provide for the study of people, places, and environments.

Standard 4—Individual Development and Identity *(See pages 88–89.)*
Social studies programs should include experiences that provide for the study of individual development and identity.

Standard 5—Individuals, Groups, and Institutions *(See pages 90–91.)*
Social studies programs should include experiences that provide for the study of individuals, groups, and institutions.

Standard 6—Power, Authority, and Governance *(See pages 93–94.)*
Social studies programs should include experiences that provide for the study of how people create and change structures of power, authority, and governance.

Standard 7—Production, Distribution, and Consumption *(See pages 95–96.)*
Social studies programs should include experiences that provide for the study of how people organize for the production, distribution, and consumption of goods and services.

Standard 8—Science, Technology, and Society *(See pages 97–98.)*
Social studies programs should include experiences that provide for the study of relationships among science, technology, and society.

Standard 9—Global Connections *(See pages 100–101.)*
Social studies programs should include experiences that provide for the study of global connections and interdependence.

Standard 10—Civic Ideals and Practices *(See pages 102–103.)*
Social studies programs should include experiences that provide for the study of the ideals, principles, and practices of citizenship in a democratic republic.

Name _____   Date _____

New Year's Traditions

Culture

DIRECTIONS: People all over the world celebrate New Year's Day. Read about some of the traditions found in different countries below. Then, answer the questions.

Brazil: Most people in Brazil wear white clothes on New Year's Eve. They do this to bring them good luck and peace for the following year. If they live near the beach, they will jump seven waves and throw flowers into the sea while making a wish. This is believed to bring good luck and fortune.

China: The Chinese celebrate the new year in late January or early February. They eat dumplings on New Year's Eve for good luck. They also hang paper cuttings. They hope this will scare away evil spirits and bring them good luck for the new year.

Spain: One tradition is to eat 12 grapes at midnight. They eat one grape each time the clock chimes. This tradition began after a big grape harvest when the king of Spain decided to give grapes to everyone to eat on New Year's Eve.

United States: There are many different traditions in the United States. Many people in the South eat black-eyed peas and turnip greens on New Year's Day. The peas represent copper and the turnip greens represent dollars. This is believed to bring good luck and wealth in the new year.

1. In what country do they eat 12 grapes as the clock strikes midnight on New Year's Eve?
   - (A) Brazil
   - (B) China
   - (C) Spain
   - (D) United States

2. If you live in Brazil, what color would you wear on New Year's Eve?
   - (F) white
   - (G) red
   - (H) blue
   - (J) green

3. Which country celebrates the new year in late January or early February?
   - (A) Brazil
   - (B) China
   - (C) Spain
   - (D) United States

4. From these passages, what seems to be the purpose of most New Year's traditions?
   - (F) to eat different foods
   - (G) to bring good luck
   - (H) to wear special clothes
   - (J) to scare away evil spirits

Social Studies

| 1.0 |

Adaptation of Native Peoples to Their Environment

Culture

DIRECTIONS: Different Native American cultures developed in different environments. Read about five of these cultures below. Then, answer the questions.

Native Americans of the Eastern Forests: This environment had plenty of rain. The summers were especially warm and rainy. It had large, lush forests. It also had lots of lakes and streams that were home to many fish and game. The Native Americans planted corn, pumpkin, squash, beans, tobacco, and gourds. They did not need to search for wild food.

Native Americans of the Plains: This environment had rolling, grassy prairie lands but few trees. The trees grew mainly beside rivers. Large herds of animals such as elk, deer, antelope, and buffalo grazed on the prairie. The tribes followed the herds across the plains.

Native Americans of the Southwest: This environment was high and dry. Most of the rain fell in the summer, when it could help plants grow. Winter snow from the mountains supplied water for streams, springs, and water holes. The Pueblos used this water to grow their food.

Native Americans of the Northwest: This environment had heavy rainfall along the northern Pacific coast. The ocean and the rivers were full of fish. It had tall, dense forests. The people gathered bulbs, berries, and seeds.

Native Americans of the Far North: This environment was frozen under ice and snow for at least half of the year. Most vegetables would not grow here. There were very few trees.

1. What was the main source of food for Native Americans of the Plains?

   (A)   elk, deer, antelope, and buffalo

   (B)   cows, pigs, and chickens

   (C)   fish and Arctic sea and land animals

   (D)   wheat and fruit

2. Which of the following used water from the mountains to help them grow their food?

   (F)   Native Americans of the Eastern Forests

   (G)   Native Americans of the Far North

   (H)   Native Americans of the Southwest

   (J)   Native Americans of the Northwest

3. Which of the following do you think were least likely to be export fishers?

   (A)   Native Americans of the Northwest

   (B)   Native Americans of the Southwest

   (C)   Native Americans of the Far North

   (D)   Native Americans of the Eastern Forests

4. Which of the following do you think were most likely to be expert farmers?

   (F)   Native Americans of the Plains

   (G)   Native Americans of the Far North

   (H)   Native Americans of the Northwest

   (J)   Native Americans of the Eastern Forests

Social Studies
2.0

Using Time Lines

Time, Continuity, and Change

DIRECTIONS: Use the following time line to answer the questions.

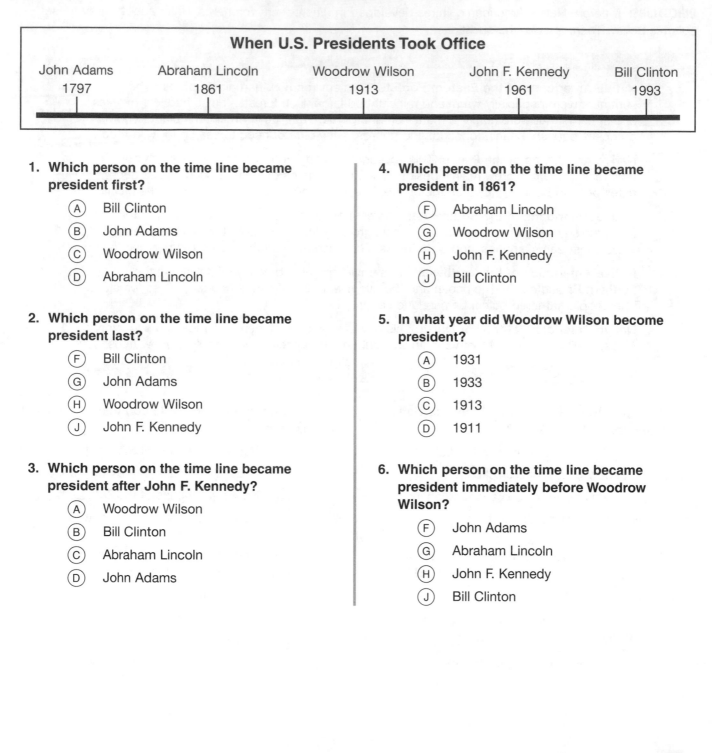

When U.S. Presidents Took Office

John Adams	Abraham Lincoln	Woodrow Wilson	John F. Kennedy	Bill Clinton
1797	1861	1913	1961	1993

1. **Which person on the time line became president first?**

   (A) Bill Clinton

   (B) John Adams

   (C) Woodrow Wilson

   (D) Abraham Lincoln

2. **Which person on the time line became president last?**

   (F) Bill Clinton

   (G) John Adams

   (H) Woodrow Wilson

   (J) John F. Kennedy

3. **Which person on the time line became president after John F. Kennedy?**

   (A) Woodrow Wilson

   (B) Bill Clinton

   (C) Abraham Lincoln

   (D) John Adams

4. **Which person on the time line became president in 1861?**

   (F) Abraham Lincoln

   (G) Woodrow Wilson

   (H) John F. Kennedy

   (J) Bill Clinton

5. **In what year did Woodrow Wilson become president?**

   (A) 1931

   (B) 1933

   (C) 1913

   (D) 1911

6. **Which person on the time line became president immediately before Woodrow Wilson?**

   (F) John Adams

   (G) Abraham Lincoln

   (H) John F. Kennedy

   (J) Bill Clinton

Social Studies

2.0

Studying the Past

Time, Continuity, and Change

DIRECTIONS: Read the following diary entries. Then, answer the questions.

> **April 27, 1856** We started West from Independence [Missouri] today. Pa has already made us lighten the wagon load. We have two oxen that are pulling it. We will be following the Oregon Trail. Pa says it will take us five to six months to reach Oregon.
>
> **May 4** We have settled into our routine. We are up at 5 A.M. and make camp for the night at 6 P.M. By 9 P.M., we are in bed—which many times is just sleeping on the ground. There's not much room in the wagon, so we walk most of the way. My little sister gets to ride more than the rest of us. Pa says we travel about 15 miles a day.
>
> **May 15** The weather was cold. Had trouble crossing the river, but we and the wagon made it. There was plenty of wood for the fire and grass for the oxen. The number of buffalo we see along the Platte River is amazing. Made 11 miles today.
>
> **June 7** We arrived in Fort Laramie [Wyoming]. We've been traveling for 6 weeks. The Rocky Mountains are ahead of us. We bought some new supplies, but they were very expensive. We were able to post a letter to Grandpa and Grandma. I fear we shall never see them again, as I doubt we shall ever return East.

1. **What is being described in the diary entries?**
   - (A) a typical family vacation in the 1850s
   - (B) a journey west along the Oregon Trail
   - (C) life at a fort in the 1850s
   - (D) the postal service in the 1850s

2. **What form of transportation did this family use to travel along the trail?**
   - (F) They rode in a boat along the river.
   - (G) They rode in a train that followed the trail.
   - (H) They rode in a wagon pulled by oxen, and walked.
   - (J) They rode on horses.

3. **How long did the typical journey take from Missouri to Oregon?**
   - (A) 5 to 6 months
   - (B) 6 weeks
   - (C) 4 months
   - (D) 15 months

4. **Which of the following resources would you use to find the locations of the places mentioned in the diary?**
   - (F) dictionary
   - (G) collection of photos of the Old West
   - (H) map
   - (J) newspaper

5. **Describe two things that you learned about life on the journey West.**

   _____

   _____

   _____

   _____

   _____

   _____

   _____

Identifying Major
U.S. Rivers and Mountains

People, Places, and Environment

DIRECTIONS: Each of the following rivers and mountain ranges are identified with a number on the map below. Match the names of the rivers and mountains with the numbers on the map.

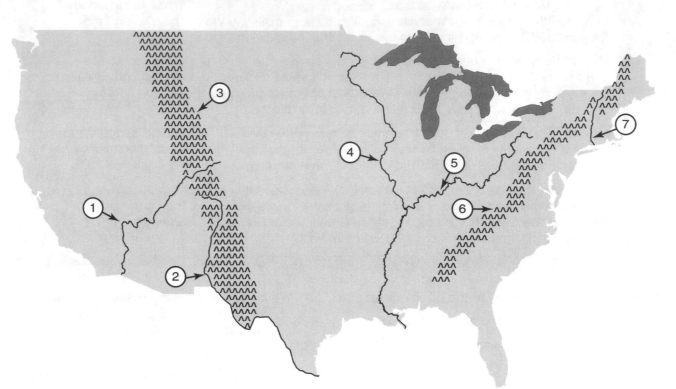

_____ 1.   **A. Mississippi River**

_____ 2.   **B. Rocky Mountains**

_____ 3.   **C. Appalachian Mountains**

_____ 4.   **D. Hudson River**

_____ 5.   **E. Rio Grande River**

_____ 6.   **F. Ohio River**

_____ 7.   **G. Colorado River**

Social Studies

| 3.0 |

Lines of
Latitude and Longitude
People, Places, and Environment

DIRECTIONS: Use the maps below to answer the questions.

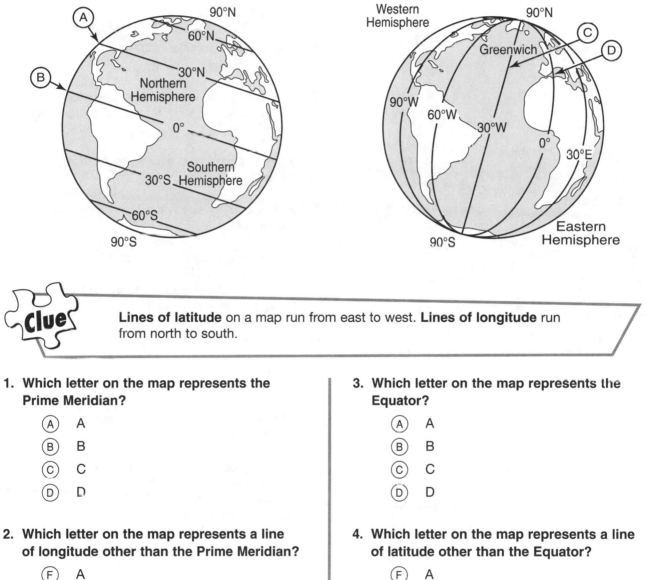

Clue   **Lines of latitude** on a map run from east to west. **Lines of longitude** run from north to south.

1. **Which letter on the map represents the Prime Meridian?**

      Ⓐ   A
      Ⓑ   B
      Ⓒ   C
      Ⓓ   D

2. **Which letter on the map represents a line of longitude other than the Prime Meridian?**

      Ⓕ   A
      Ⓖ   B
      Ⓗ   C
      Ⓙ   D

3. **Which letter on the map represents the Equator?**

      Ⓐ   A
      Ⓑ   B
      Ⓒ   C
      Ⓓ   D

4. **Which letter on the map represents a line of latitude other than the Equator?**

      Ⓕ   A
      Ⓖ   B
      Ⓗ   C
      Ⓙ   D

Social Studies

3.0

Identifying
Geographic Features

People, Places, and Environment

DIRECTIONS: Match the geographic feature in Column A with its description in Column B.

Column A

_____ **1.** bay

_____ **2.** canyon

_____ **3.** gulf

_____ **4.** glacier

_____ **5.** island

_____ **6.** lake

_____ **7.** plain

_____ **8.** mountain

_____ **9.** ocean

_____ **10.** peninsula

_____ **11.** plateau

_____ **12.** river

Column B

A. a large, flat area of land that is higher than the surrounding land

B. a body of water that is part of the sea or ocean and reaches into land; it is usually larger than a bay

C. a piece of land that is completely surrounded by water

D. a large body of salt water that surrounds a continent

E. a deep valley with very steep sides

F. a high, steeply sloped area formed by the upward movement of rock

G. a large mass of slowly moving ice

H. a large body of water surrounded by land on all sides

I. a broad, flat, or gently rolling area that usually has a low elevation

J. a moving body of water that usually empties into a lake, the sea, or the ocean

K. a body of land that is surrounded by water on three sides

L. a body of water that is partly surrounded by the land

Social Studies

| 1.0–3.0 |

For pages 80–86

Mini-Test 1

Culture; Time, Continuity, and Change;
People, Places, and Environment

DIRECTIONS: Choose the best answer.

1. **In which of the following countries do the people eat dumplings and hang paper cuttings on New Year's Eve?**
   - (A) Brazil
   - (B) China
   - (C) Spain
   - (D) United States

DIRECTIONS: Use the information in the time line below to answer questions 2–4.

1803: Thomas Jefferson makes the Louisiana Purchase
1804: Lewis and Clark begin their journey to the West
1840s: Start of the great migration westward on the California and Oregon Trails
1848: Gold is discovered in California

2. **When did the great migration westward begin?**
   - (F) before Lewis and Clark's journey and after gold was discovered in California
   - (G) after the Louisiana Purchase and before Lewis and Clark's journey
   - (H) after Lewis and Clark's journey and before the Louisiana Purchase
   - (J) after Lewis and Clark's journey and before gold was discovered in California

3. **In what year was gold discovered in California?**
   - (A) 1848
   - (B) 1804
   - (C) 1884
   - (D) 1840

4. **What event occurred first on the time line?**
   - (F) Lewis and Clark's journey
   - (G) Louisiana Purchase
   - (H) discovery of gold in California
   - (J) great migration westward

DIRECTIONS: Choose the best answer.

5. **Which of the following rivers is the longest in the United States?**
   - (A) Rio Grande
   - (B) Colorado
   - (C) Ohio
   - (D) Mississippi

6. **What would you find at 0° longitude on a globe?**
   - (F) the North Pole
   - (G) the South Pole
   - (H) the Equator
   - (J) the Prime Meridian

7. **A part of a sea or ocean that reaches into land, usually larger than a bay, is a _____ .**
   - (A) river
   - (B) gulf
   - (C) lake
   - (D) peninsula

8. **A broad, flat, or gently rolling area, usually low in elevation, is a _____ .**
   - (F) plain
   - (G) plateau
   - (H) peninsula
   - (J) canyon

Name _____   Date _____

Personal Changes

Individual Development and Identity

DIRECTIONS: Think about some of the changes you have experienced or new things you have recently tried to do. For example, have you grown taller or stronger? Can you run faster than you used to? Are you becoming a better reader? Have you started playing a new sport or gotten better at one? Have you learned a new skill or started a new hobby? Have you moved to a new neighborhood or school? Have you made a new group of friends? Pick one of these changes or areas of interest. Then, write a few paragraphs about how this has made a difference in your life.

STOP

Social Studies

| 4.0 |

Family Traditions

Individual Development and Identity

DIRECTIONS: Family traditions are something your family does to celebrate special days or moments. Read the following story about one family's birthday traditions. Then, in the space below, describe one of the traditions that you have in your family.

> I woke up this morning and remembered it was my birthday! I was so excited. I couldn't wait for the day to get started. I jumped out of bed and ran to the kitchen. I knew Mom would be making my favorite breakfast. Sure enough, she was mixing up the batter for some waffles. Yum! Soon, everyone in my family was sitting at the kitchen table, eating waffles with whipped cream and blueberry sauce. As soon as breakfast was done, my sister and I quickly left for school.
>
> While I was at school, my mom decorated the family room. She put colorful balloons all around the room. Then, she hung streamers and a Happy Birthday! banner. She stacked all of my presents in front of the fireplace. She made my favorite cake with lots of chocolate frosting.
>
> When I got home, the house looked just as I had imagined it. As soon as my dad got home, everyone helped make my favorite dinner. Everyone, that is, except me! I didn't have to help because it was my birthday. After we ate hamburgers and corn on the cob, we went into the family room. This was my favorite part of the whole day—opening my presents. I took my time unwrapping each one because I wanted this part to last. After I opened my last gift, my mom came into the room carrying the cake with all of the candles lit. As my family sang the "Happy Birthday" song, I pretended to be embarrassed. But I really did like it. It was a great day!

_____

_____

_____

_____

_____

_____

_____

_____

_____

_____

_____

_____

Name _____ Date _____

Roles in Groups

Individuals, Groups, and Institutions

DIRECTIONS: As members of groups, we are expected to act in certain ways. These are the roles we have within these groups. Think about some of the groups you are a member of, such as your class at school, family, sports team, clubs, special groups at church, and so on. Choose two of these groups. Then, think about the following questions: What are your responsibilities in these groups? How do you help out in these groups? How would other members in these groups describe what you do? Then, write the names of your groups on the lines below and describe your role in each of them.

Group 1 _____

_____

_____

_____

_____

_____

_____

_____

_____

_____

_____

Group 2 _____

_____

_____

_____

_____

_____

_____

_____

_____

_____

_____

_____

STOP

Social Studies

5.0

Institutions

Individuals, Groups, and Institutions

DIRECTIONS: Choose the best answer.

Clue

An **institution** is an organization or business. Each institution provides a different type of service. Schools, hospitals, banks, and churches are all examples of institutions.

1. **Providing education is the main role of which of the following institutions?**

   (A) hospitals

   (B) schools

   (C) churches

   (D) the government

2. **Providing health care is the main role of which of the following institutions?**

   (F) schools

   (G) courts

   (H) hospitals

   (J) churches

3. **Providing worship services is the main role of which of the following institutions?**

   (A) churches

   (B) hospitals

   (C) schools

   (D) police stations

4. **What is the purpose of a local food bank?**

   (F) to collect food for use during emergencies

   (G) to provide groceries to the poor

   (H) to provide cash in exchange for food

   (J) to provide food in exchange for cash

5. **Which of the following institutions helps to protect the people in your community?**

   (A) the police

   (B) the local food bank

   (C) the bank

   (D) the school

6. **You are hurt while playing in a soccer game and need to have your leg X-rayed. Which of the following institutions could help you?**

   (F) the bank

   (G) the library

   (H) the police station

   (J) the hospital

7. **You need to do some research for a school project. Which of the following institutions could help you?**

   (A) the bank

   (B) the library

   (C) a local church

   (D) the hospital

8. **Your parents want to buy a new house. Which of the following institutions could help them get a loan to pay for the house?**

   (F) the bank

   (G) the library

   (H) the police station

   (J) the hospital

STOP

Social Studies

4.0–5.0

For pages 88–91

Mini-Test 2

Individual Development and Identity;
Individuals, Groups, and Institutions

DIRECTIONS: Choose the best answer.

1. **Which of the following changes have you most likely experienced in the past year?**

   Ⓐ You are taller.

   Ⓑ You are shorter.

   Ⓒ Your eye color has changed.

   Ⓓ Your hair color has changed.

2. **Which of the following is not an example of a personal change?**

   Ⓕ You started playing a new sport.

   Ⓖ You like to go to movies.

   Ⓗ You are becoming a better reader.

   Ⓙ You moved to a new town.

3. **You can run faster than you used to. This change might help your ability to play which of the following sports?**

   Ⓐ basketball

   Ⓑ soccer

   Ⓒ football

   Ⓓ all of the above

4. **A practice or celebration that is unique to your family may be called a(n) _____ .**

   Ⓕ superstition

   Ⓖ tradition

   Ⓗ trait

   Ⓙ oddity

5. **Paying attention in class is one behavior expected of you in your role as a _____ .**

   Ⓐ coach

   Ⓑ student

   Ⓒ family member

   Ⓓ club leader

6. **As a member of a sports team, you are expected to _____ .**

   Ⓕ attend practices

   Ⓖ listen to your coach

   Ⓗ participate in the games

   Ⓙ all of the above

7. **Which of the following services does a hospital provide?**

   Ⓐ savings plan

   Ⓑ education

   Ⓒ health care

   Ⓓ transportation

8. **Which of the following institutions would you go to for entertainment?**

   Ⓕ cinema

   Ⓖ theater

   Ⓗ symphony

   Ⓙ all of the above

9. **Which of the following services does a bank provide?**

   Ⓐ savings plan

   Ⓑ education

   Ⓒ entertainment

   Ⓓ transportation

Social Studies

6.0

Rights and Responsibilities

Power, Authority, and Governance

DIRECTIONS: Read the definitions below. Then, use the definitions to help you choose the best answer.

A *right*, or *freedom*, is something the law says that you can have or do. It usually applies to all people in a society or group. Some very important rights that all American citizens have are listed in the Bill of Rights. One example of a right that all Americans have is the right to free speech.

A *responsibility* is a duty or a job that you have. All citizens of the United States have certain responsibilities. For example, a responsibility of all American citizens is to obey the law. You also have responsibilities in other areas of your life, such as at school or at home. One example of a responsibility you might have at home is to clean your room.

---

1. As a student, you have the _____ to vote for the class president.

    (A) right

    (B) responsibility

2. Learning everything you can about the candidates for class president before you vote is a _____ .

    (F) right

    (G) responsibility

3. Your family attends a religious service each week. This is an example of a _____ .

    (A) right

    (B) responsibility

4. Your parents pay taxes on all of the money they earn. This is an example of a _____ .

    (F) right

    (G) responsibility

5. Your mom receives a letter asking her to report for jury duty. This is an example of a _____ .

    (A) right

    (B) responsibility

6. Wearing clothes that follow your school's dress code is an example of a _____ .

    (F) right

    (G) responsibility

7. One of your chores at home is to take out the trash. This is an example of a _____ .

    (A) right

    (B) responsibility

8. When you are riding in a car, the driver of the car must obey the traffic laws. This is an example of a _____ .

    (F) right

    (G) responsibility

9. Doing your homework is a _____ .

    (A) right

    (B) responsibility

10. You have the _____ to receive an education.

    (F) right

    (G) responsibility

STOP

Name _____ Date _____

6.0

Levels and Branches of Government

Powers, Authority, and Governance

DIRECTIONS: Look at the table below. It shows the levels and branches of government in the United States. Use the table to help you answer the questions.

Levels of Government	Branches of Government	Leaders of This Branch	This branch of government is responsible for . . .
National	Executive	President of the United States	. . . making sure laws are obeyed.
	Legislative	Congress	. . . making laws.
	Judicial	U.S. Supreme Court	. . . interpreting and explaining the laws.
State	Executive	Governor of the state	. . . making sure laws are obeyed.
	Legislative	General Assembly or State Legislature	. . . making laws.
	Judicial	State Courts	. . . interpreting and explaining the laws.
Local	Executive	Mayor	. . . making sure laws are obeyed.
	Legislative	City Council or City Commissioners	. . . making laws.
	Judicial	Municipal and County Courts	. . . interpreting and explaining the laws.

1. **Which of the following is not one of the three levels of U.S. government?**

   Ⓐ national

   Ⓑ local

   Ⓒ state

   Ⓓ judicial

2. **Which of the following is not one of the three branches of government?**

   Ⓕ executive

   Ⓖ legislative

   Ⓗ state

   Ⓙ judicial

3. **The judicial branch is responsible for _____ .**

   Ⓐ making laws

   Ⓑ interpreting and explaining laws

   Ⓒ making sure laws are obeyed

   Ⓓ changing laws

4. **In state government, the leaders of the legislative branch are _____ .**

   Ⓕ the governor

   Ⓖ the General Assembly or State Legislature

   Ⓗ the mayor

   Ⓙ the city council

5. **The executive branch is responsible for _____ .**

   Ⓐ making laws

   Ⓑ interpreting and explaining laws

   Ⓒ making sure laws are obeyed

   Ⓓ changing laws

6. **In the national government, the leader of the executive branch is _____ .**

   Ⓕ Congress

   Ⓖ the Supreme Court

   Ⓗ the Senate

   Ⓙ the President

Name _____ Date _____

7.0

Identifying Needs Versus Wants

Production, Distribution, and Consumption

DIRECTIONS: For each of the following items, write **N** if it is an example of a need or **W** if it is an example of a want.

Examples:

A **need** is something you must have in order to be able to live or survive. An example of a need is water.

A **want** is something you would like to have, but you do not need it in order to live or survive. An example of a want is a new bike.

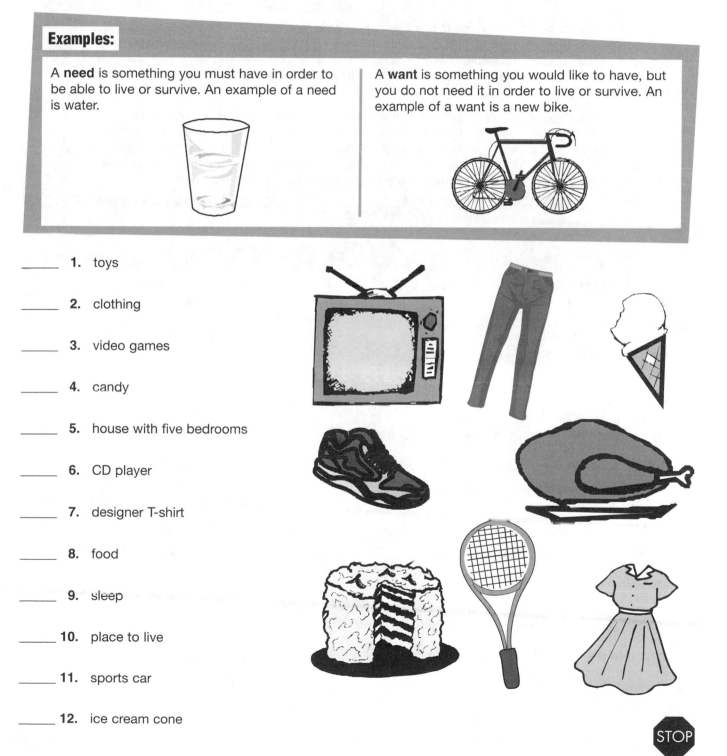

_____ **1.** toys

_____ **2.** clothing

_____ **3.** video games

_____ **4.** candy

_____ **5.** house with five bedrooms

_____ **6.** CD player

_____ **7.** designer T-shirt

_____ **8.** food

_____ **9.** sleep

_____ **10.** place to live

_____ **11.** sports car

_____ **12.** ice cream cone

STOP

Social Studies

8.0

Public vs. Private Goods and Services

Production, Distribution, and Consumption

DIRECTIONS: Read the definitions below and look at the chart. Then, answer the questions.

A **private good** or **service** is one that can be sold to people. The one who benefits is the person who bought the item or service. A private good or service can be used by only one person at a time. Once the item or service is sold, no one else can buy it. An example of a private good or service is a banana. The only person who benefits from the banana is the buyer.

A **public good** or **service** is one that is used by all of the people in a community, whether or not they paid for it. These goods or services help everyone in the community. The government provides us with public goods and services. Public goods and services are paid for by taxes. An example of a public good or service is police protection. The people who benefit from the police protection are all of the people that live in a community.

Examples:

Private Goods and Services:	Public Goods or Services:
• Food	• Armed forces (army, navy, air force, marines)
• Clothing	• Fire protection
• School supplies	• Street and highway repair and upkeep
• Dinner at a restaurant	• Library
• Haircut	• Schools
• Movie ticket	• Snow removal
• Car repair	• Post office
• Dry cleaning	

1. **Public goods and services _____ .**

   Ⓐ help only the people who are able to pay for them

   Ⓑ help everyone in a society

   Ⓒ can be used by only one person at a time

   Ⓓ are no longer available once they are used

2. **Which of the following is a public service?**

   Ⓕ grocery stores

   Ⓖ hair salons

   Ⓗ movie theaters

   Ⓙ schools

3. **Private goods and services _____ .**

   Ⓐ can be used by everyone in a community

   Ⓑ are paid for by taxes

   Ⓒ help only the people who are able to pay for them

   Ⓓ are provided by the government

4. **Which of the following is a private service?**

   Ⓕ police protection

   Ⓖ street repair

   Ⓗ lawn care

   Ⓙ snow removal

Social Studies

| 8.0 |

Impact of Inventions

Science, Technology, and Society

DIRECTIONS: Choose the best answer.

1. **Which of the following inventions made it possible to create printed materials more quickly?**
   - (A) telephone
   - (B) printing press
   - (C) steam engine
   - (D) telegraph

2. **Which of the following inventions made housework easier?**
   - (F) telephone
   - (G) automobile
   - (H) dishwasher
   - (J) cotton gin

3. **Which of the following inventions would best help you do research for a school report?**
   - (A) computer
   - (B) CD player
   - (C) radio
   - (D) television

4. **Which of the following inventions helped people travel more quickly from place to place?**
   - (F) airplane
   - (G) automobile
   - (H) steam locomotive
   - (J) all of the above

5. **Which of the following inventions made it easier for people to live and work in tall buildings?**
   - (A) electric lightbulb
   - (B) telephone
   - (C) elevator

   - (D) vacuum cleaner

6. **Which of the following inventions help farmers protect their crops from cattle?**
   - (F) windmill
   - (G) barbed wire
   - (H) steel plow
   - (J) cotton gin

7. **Which of the following inventions did not help improve how people communicate?**
   - (A) telegraph
   - (B) telephone
   - (C) telescope
   - (D) television

8. **Which of the following inventions made it possible for people to see better at night?**
   - (F) television
   - (G) automobile
   - (H) telescope
   - (J) electric lightbulb

9. **The automobile was an important invention. It was one of the reasons that people were able to move from the cities to the suburbs. Why do you think this is so?**

   _____

   _____

   _____

   _____

   _____

   _____

   _____

STOP

Name _____ Date _____

Changes in the Rain Forest

Science, Technology, and Society

DIRECTIONS: Read the following passage. Then, answer the questions.

Rain forests all over the world are being cleared, or cut down. They can be cleared quickly by using chainsaws or bulldozers. Sometimes, fires are set in order to clear them.

Rain forests are cleared for different reasons. They might be cleared for the trees. The wood from the trees is used in products such as furniture and paper. At other times, they are cleared for the land. The land is then used for growing crops or raising animals for food.

We have learned that there are problems with destroying the rain forests. One problem is erosion. When the trees are removed, the roots are no longer there to hold the soil in place. This causes the soil to erode, or wear away. Heavy equipment is used to cut down and move the logs to other places. Driving this equipment back and forth on the land also causes the soil to break down and wash away. Another problem is pollution. The heavy equipment creates air and water pollution. Fires used to burn down the trees cause air pollution.

Rain forests are home to millions of plants, animals, and insects. Researchers have found plants in the rain forest that can be used to make medicines. They are concerned that these plants will disappear before more discoveries are made. These natural resources could be used to prevent or heal diseases. This would be worth more than the lumber from the trees or the income from farming and ranching.

1. **Which of the following tools is used to help clear the rain forests?**

   Ⓐ axe

   Ⓑ chainsaw

   Ⓒ handsaw

   Ⓓ lathe

2. **How does clearing rain forests affect pollution?**

   Ⓕ It decreases air and water pollution.

   Ⓖ It increases air and water pollution.

   Ⓗ It has no effect on pollution.

   Ⓙ It helps to prevent pollution.

3. **How is the soil in the rain forest affected when trees are removed?**

   Ⓐ The soil erodes and washes away.

   Ⓑ The soil builds up.

   Ⓒ The amount of soil stays the same.

   Ⓓ none of the above

4. **How is the land used after the trees are cleared from the rain forest?**

   Ⓕ It is used for farming.

   Ⓖ It is used for ranching.

   Ⓗ It is used for both farming and ranching.

   Ⓙ The land is not used for other purposes.

5. **Describe why we might not want to continue to clear the rain forests.**

   _____

   _____

   _____

   _____

   _____

   _____

   _____

   _____

Social Studies

| 6.0–8.0 |

For pages 93–98

Mini-Test 3

Powers, Authority, and Governance; Production, Distribution, and Consumption; Science, Technology, and Society

DIRECTIONS: Choose the best answer.

1. **Rights are _____ that are given to all people in a society or group.**
   - (A) duties
   - (B) freedoms
   - (C) responsibilities
   - (D) privileges

2. **Paying taxes is a _____ .**
   - (F) right
   - (G) responsibility
   - (H) freedom
   - (J) privilege

3. **The United States has _____ branches of government.**
   - (A) one
   - (B) two
   - (C) three
   - (D) four

4. **Which of the following is a branch of the U.S. government?**
   - (F) representative
   - (G) executive
   - (H) direct
   - (J) financial

5. **Which of the following is not a level of government?**
   - (A) local
   - (B) state
   - (C) national
   - (D) judicial

6. **Something you must have in order to live is called a _____ .**
   - (F) good
   - (G) want
   - (H) need
   - (J) service

7. **A portable CD player is an example of a _____ .**
   - (A) need
   - (B) service
   - (C) distribution
   - (D) want

8. **The government provides _____ goods and services that help everyone in society.**
   - (F) public
   - (G) private
   - (H) beneficial
   - (J) humanitarian

9. **Public goods and services are paid for by _____ .**
   - (A) individuals
   - (B) taxes
   - (C) donations
   - (D) loans

10. **The invention of the automobile and airplane helped improve _____ .**
    - (F) communication
    - (G) work life
    - (H) transportation
    - (J) farming

STOP

Social Studies

| 9.0 |

Nonverbal Communication

Global Connections

DIRECTIONS: You communicate with people all the time without saying any words. This is called *nonverbal communication*. You can communicate by using different gestures. This includes the way you look at someone, the way you place your body, or the way you use your hands. Study the table below about nonverbal communication. Then, answer the questions.

Gesture	What It Means in the United States	What It Means in Other Countries
nod your head up and down	• yes	• In Bulgaria and Greece, it means *no*.
wave your hand with your palm facing outward	• hello or good-bye • you want to get someone's attention	• In Europe, it can mean *no*.
form a circle with your thumb and index finger	• OK	• In France, it means *zero* or *worthless*. • In Japan, it means *money*.
smile	• you are happy • you think something is funny	• In Asia, it can mean you are happy, angry, confused, sad, or are apologizing.
point your index finger near your ear and make circles	• crazy	• In Argentina, it means you have a telephone call.
hold your thumb up while closing the rest of your fingers in a fist	• good job	• In Germany and Japan, it means *one*.

1. **If you want to tell a person in Greece "no," which gesture should you make?**

   (A) shake head side to side

   (B) hold your thumb up

   (C) nod head up and down

   (D) smile

2. **If you form a circle with your thumb and index finger, what may someone from France think you are saying?**

   (F) good-bye

   (G) OK

   (H) you are worthless

   (J) you have a telephone call

3. **How could you tell a sales clerk in Japan that you would like one item?**

   (A) hold your thumb up

   (B) hold your index finger up

   (C) nod your head up and down once

   (D) none of the above

4. **If you wave your hand with the palm facing outward, what might a person in Europe think you are saying?**

   (F) hello

   (G) no

   (H) good-bye

   (J) yes

STOP

Social Studies

Conflict, Cooperation, and Interdependence

Global Connections

DIRECTIONS: Choose the best answer.

> **Conflict** is when people or groups disagree. Conflicts happen when people have different needs, wants, or demands.
>
> **Cooperation** is when people work together. This often results in both sides being helped by working together.
>
> **Interdependence** is when people or groups rely on each other to help meet some of their needs.

1. **On Saturday morning, you want to spend your time building a model. Your mom wants you to clean your room. This is an example of _____ .**

   Ⓐ interdependence

   Ⓑ cooperation

   Ⓒ conflict

   Ⓓ all of the above

2. **Your mom says she will help you build your model in the morning if you help her clean your room in the afternoon. This is an example of _____ .**

   Ⓕ cooperation

   Ⓖ interdependence

   Ⓗ conflict

   Ⓙ none of the above

3. **You want to learn to play the piano. A woman in your neighborhood gives piano lessons. Your parents hire her to be your piano teacher. You get the lessons you want and your teacher is paid for her service. This is an example of _____ .**

   Ⓐ interdependence

   Ⓑ cooperation

   Ⓒ conflict

   Ⓓ none of the above

4. **Country A has oranges, but it needs oil. Country B has oil, but it needs oranges. Country A sells oranges to Country B, and Country B sells oil to Country A. This is an example of _____ .**

   Ⓕ conflict

   Ⓖ cooperation

   Ⓗ interdependence

   Ⓙ all of the above

5. **Your sports team has just held a fundraiser. Half of the team members want to use the money for new uniforms. The other half wants to use the money for new equipment. This is an example of _____ .**

   Ⓐ conflict

   Ⓑ cooperation

   Ⓒ interdependence

   Ⓓ none of the above

6. **A high school basketball team and volleyball team decide to have a car wash to raise money. They agree to equally divide the money that is earned between the teams. This is an example of _____ .**

   Ⓕ interdependence

   Ⓖ conflict

   Ⓗ cooperation

   Ⓙ all of the above

Social Studies

10.0

Traits of Historic Figures

Civic Ideals and Practices

DIRECTIONS: Read the passage. Then, answer the questions.

Paul Revere was born in Boston, Massachusetts, in 1735. He became a silversmith. This means he worked with gold and silver. He made items such as spoons and tea sets. Later, he became a dentist.

In 1765, the British started to tax the colonists. This made the colonists angry. After this happened, Revere joined some secret patriot groups. A *patriot* is someone who supports and defends his country. One of the groups he joined was called the *Sons of Liberty*.

Revere was a very good horse rider. As a result, he was often asked to carry messages to the patriot groups. He would ride his horse between Boston, New York, and Philadelphia.

In 1773, Revere joined with others in the Boston Tea Party. Colonists had to pay taxes on tea to the British. To show that they did not like these taxes, they threw the tea into Boston Harbor. Revere later rode to New York and Philadelphia. He told the patriots in those cities about what had happened in Boston.

On April 18, 1775, Revere was told to ride to Lexington. He had to warn two men that the British were coming to arrest them. He also warned that the British were planning to attack. Revere rode from Boston to Lexington. He delivered both of the messages. Then, he rode with two other men to another town in Massachusetts. The British captured all three riders, but they were released.

Revere later became an officer. He fought against the British in the Revolutionary War. When the war was over, he went back to being a silversmith. He died in 1818.

---

1. **A patriot is someone who _____ .**

   (A) works with gold and silver

   (B) delivers messages

   (C) fought for the British

   (D) supports and defends his country

2. **What was a major role that Revere filled with the patriot organizations?**

   (F) He made false teeth for patriots.

   (G) He was a messenger between patriot organizations.

   (H) He protested high British taxes.

   (J) He was a silversmith.

3. **Which of the following words is a synonym for *liberty*?**

   (A) cooperation

   (B) respect

   (C) freedom

   (D) happiness

4. **Which of the following is a way Revere demonstrated the importance of liberty in his life?**

   (F) He joined patriot organizations.

   (G) He warned colonists of a planned British attack.

   (H) He fought in the Revolutionary War.

   (J) all of the above

STOP

Name _____ Date _____

Social Studies

| 10.0 |

Freedoms of Expression

Civic Ideals and Practices

DIRECTIONS: Read the passage. Then, answer the questions.

First Amendment Rights

The First Amendment to the U.S. Constitution gives Americans several freedoms. One is the freedom of religion. This means that Americans have the right to practice any religion they want. The other freedoms are called *freedoms of expression*. Two of these freedoms give people the right to speak or write freely and the government will not try to stop them. These are called *freedom of speech* and *freedom of the press*. The freedom of assembly allows people to meet together. The meetings should be peaceful and legal. The freedom to petition gives people the right to ask the government to help correct a wrong that has been done to them. One way this can be done is by going to court.

1. **Which of the following is not one of the freedoms of expression?**

   (A) freedom to petition

   (B) freedom of assembly

   (C) freedom of speech

   (D) freedom of religion

2. **Which of the following freedoms allows people to have their opinions printed in the newspaper?**

   (F) freedom of religion

   (G) freedom of the press

   (H) freedom of assembly

   (J) freedom to petition

3. **Your class wants to meet at the public park for a picnic. Your right to do this is protected under _____ .**

   (A) freedom of assembly

   (B) freedom of speech

   (C) freedom of religion

   (D) freedom to petition

4. **You want to tell a group of people why you support your candidate for mayor. The right to do this is covered under _____ .**

   (F) freedom of the press

   (G) freedom to religion

   (H) freedom of speech

   (J) freedom of assembly

5. **You got hurt when you used a certain product. Which of the following freedoms allows you to file a lawsuit against the company that made the product you used?**

   (A) freedom of speech

   (B) freedom of the press

   (C) freedom to petition

   (D) freedom of assembly

6. **Which amendment gives us our freedoms of expression?**

   (F) Fifth Amendment

   (G) Third Amendment

   (H) First Amendment

   (J) Fourth Amendment

Social Studies

9.0–10.0

For pages 100–103

Mini-Test 4

Global Connections; Civic Ideals and Practices

DIRECTIONS: Choose the best answer.

1. **People can communicate without using words. When gestures are used to communicate, they _____ .**

    (A) mean the same thing in every country

    (B) mean the same thing only within very small groups of people

    (C) can mean different things in different countries and cultures

    (D) should always be avoided

2. **If you are in Bulgaria and nod your head up and down, it means _____ .**

    (F) yes

    (G) hello

    (H) no

    (J) zero

3. **_____ is when people work together.**

    (A) Conflict

    (B) Cooperation

    (C) Dependence

    (D) Interdependence

4. **_____ is when people have to rely on each other to help meet some of their needs.**

    (F) Independence

    (G) Cooperation

    (H) Interdependence

    (J) Conflict

5. **Paul Revere was a member of patriot organizations. He warned colonists of a British attack. He fought in the Revolutionary War. These actions show that _____ was very important to him.**

    (A) human dignity

    (B) liberty

    (C) justice

    (D) equality

6. **Which of the following freedoms allows people to gather together for peaceful and legal reasons?**

    (F) freedom of speech

    (G) freedom of assembly

    (H) freedom of religion

    (J) freedom of participation

7. **Freedom of speech, press, assembly, and petition are freedoms of _____ .**

    (A) religion

    (B) nature

    (C) expression

    (D) participation

8. **Where would you find the rights that are listed in question 7?**

    (F) in the Declaration of Independence

    (G) in the First Amendment to the U.S. Constitution

    (H) at the White House

    (J) in the Preamble to the U.S. Constitution

STOP

How Am I Doing?

Mini-Test 1 Page 87 **Number Correct** [ ]	**8** answers correct	**Great Job!** Move on to the section test on page 107.
	4–7 answers correct	**You're almost there!** But you still need a little practice. Review practice pages 80–86 before moving on to the section test on page 107.
	0–3 answers correct	**Oops!** Time to review what you have learned and try again. Review the practice section on pages 80–86. Then, retake the test on page 87. Now, move on to the section test on page 107.
Mini-Test 2 Page 92 **Number Correct** [ ]	**9** answers correct	**Awesome!** Move on to the section test on page 107.
	5–8 answers correct	**You're almost there!** But you still need a little practice. Review practice pages 88–91 before moving on to the section test on page 107.
	0–4 answers correct	**Oops!** Time to review what you have learned and try again. Review the practice section on pages 88–91. Then, retake the test on page 92. Now, move on to the section test on page 107.
Mini-Test 3 Page 99 **Number Correct** [ ]	**10** answers correct	**Great Job!** Move on to the section test on page 107.
	6–9 answers correct	**You're almost there!** But you still need a little practice. Review practice pages 93–98 before moving on to the section test on page 107.
	0–5 answers correct	**Oops!** Time to review what you have learned and try again. Review the practice section on pages 93–98. Then, retake the test on page 99. Now, move on to the section test on page 107.

How Am I Doing?

Mini-Test 4	8 answers correct	**Awesome!** Move on to the section test on page 107.
Page 104 **Number Correct**	4–7 answers correct	**You're almost there!** But you still need a little practice. Review practice pages 100–103 before moving on to the section test on page 107.
	0–3 answers correct	**Oops!** Time to review what you have learned and try again. Review the practice section on pages 100–103. Then, retake the test on page 104. Now, move on to the section test on page 107.

Final Social Studies Test
for pages 80–104

DIRECTIONS: Choose the best answer.

1. **Which of the following is a New Year's tradition in Brazil?**

    (A) wearing white clothes

    (B) hanging paper cuttings

    (C) eating 12 grapes at midnight

    (D) eating black-eyed peas and turnip greens

DIRECTIONS: Use the information in the time line bolow to answer questions 2–4.

1450: Printing press invented
1714: First typewriter invented in England
1826: First camera invented
1833: Telegraph invented
1877: Phonograph invented
1891: Motion picture camera invented

2. **What was invented before the typewriter?**

    (F) the camera

    (G) the telegraph

    (H) the printing press

    (J) the phonograph

3. **The telephone was invented in 1876. Where would it be placed on the time line?**

    (A) after the invention of the printing press and before the invention of the typewriter

    (B) after the invention of the typewriter and before the invention of the camera

    (C) after the invention of the phonograph and before the invention of the motion picture camera

    (D) after the invention of the telegraph and before the invention of the phonograph

4. **Which item was invented last on the time line?**

    (F) the phonograph

    (G) the motion picture camera

    (H) the camera

    (J) the printing press

DIRECTIONS: Choose the best answer.

5. **You are visiting the Blue Ridge Mountains in Virginia. These mountains are part of what larger mountain chain?**

    (A) Rocky Mountains

    (B) Appalachian Mountains

    (C) Sierra Nevada

    (D) Cascades

6. **Lines that go from north to south on a globe are called _____ .**

    (F) lines of latitude

    (G) lines of longitude

    (H) equators

    (J) meridians

7. **Low land between hills or mountains is a _____ .**

    (A) prairie

    (B) peninsula

    (C) mesa

    (D) valley

8. **A large body of water surrounded by land is a(n) _____ .**

    (F) bay

    (G) lake

    (H) ocean

    (J) river

GO

9. **You have experienced the following changes in the past year. Which of these changes might help you play the piano more easily?**

   Ⓐ your legs have grown longer

   Ⓑ your fingers have grown longer

   Ⓒ your eyesight has weakened

   Ⓓ you require larger meals

10. **Showing respect to your parents is one behavior that is expected of you in your role as a _____ .**

    Ⓕ student

    Ⓖ team member

    Ⓗ family member

    Ⓙ club member

11. **To which institution would you go to learn to become a teacher?**

    Ⓐ YMCA

    Ⓑ university

    Ⓒ hospital

    Ⓓ library

12. **Which of the following institutions would help you earn interest on your savings?**

    Ⓕ church

    Ⓖ school

    Ⓗ bank

    Ⓙ hospital

13. **Which institution should you contact to report a crime?**

    Ⓐ the police department

    Ⓑ city hall

    Ⓒ the library

    Ⓓ the hospital

14. **_____ can best be described as duties.**

    Ⓕ Rights

    Ⓖ Responsibilities

    Ⓗ Freedoms

    Ⓙ Privileges

15. **All American citizens over the age of 18 have the _____ to vote in an election.**

    Ⓐ right

    Ⓑ responsibility

    Ⓒ both of the above

    Ⓓ none of the above

16. **Paying off your debts is a _____ .**

    Ⓕ right

    Ⓖ responsibility

    Ⓗ privilege

    Ⓙ freedom

17. **How many levels of government are found in the United States?**

    Ⓐ two

    Ⓑ three

    Ⓒ four

    Ⓓ five

18. **How many branches of government are there in each level of government?**

    Ⓕ one

    Ⓖ two

    Ⓗ three

    Ⓙ four

19. **The president of the United States is the leader of which branch of government?**

    Ⓐ judicial

    Ⓑ legislative

    Ⓒ representative

    Ⓓ executive

GO

20. Which branch of government is responsible for making laws?

(F) executive

(G) legislative

(H) representative

(J) judicial

21. Something that you would like to have but do not have to have in order to live is a _____ .

(A) need

(B) service

(C) good

(D) want

22. Shelter is an example of a _____ .

(F) good

(G) need

(H) want

(J) service

23. Which of the following is not a public service funded through taxes?

(A) schools

(B) highways

(C) restaurants

(D) police protection

24. Which of the following is a private service?

(F) library

(G) movie theater

(H) snow removal

(J) highway repair

25. Which of the following inventions helped people to make clothing?

(A) washing machine

(B) sewing machine

(C) clothes dryer

(D) dishwasher

26. Using gestures to communicate with others is a form of _____ communication.

(F) verbal

(G) manual

(H) oral

(J) nonverbal

27. A struggle or disagreement that happens when people have different needs, wants, or demands is known as _____ .

(A) cooperation

(B) interdependence

(C) dependence

(D) conflict

28. Which of the following is not one of the freedoms of expressions?

(F) freedom of speech

(G) freedom of press

(H) freedom of assembly

(J) freedom of participation

29. Having the right to speak or write freely without the government getting involved is _____ .

(A) freedom of speech

(B) freedom of assembly

(C) freedom of religion

(D) freedom to petition

30. Having the right to practice any faith that you choose is known as _____ .

(F) freedom of speech

(G) freedom of assembly

(H) freedom of religion

(J) freedom to petition

Name _____   Date _____

Final Social Studies Test

Answer Sheet

1 (A) (B) (C) (D)
2 (F) (G) (H) (J)
3 (A) (B) (C) (D)
4 (F) (G) (H) (J)
5 (A) (B) (C) (D)
6 (F) (G) (H) (J)
7 (A) (B) (C) (D)
8 (F) (G) (H) (J)
9 (A) (B) (C) (D)
10 (F) (G) (H) (J)

11 (A) (B) (C) (D)
12 (F) (G) (H) (J)
13 (A) (B) (C) (D)
14 (F) (G) (H) (J)
15 (A) (B) (C) (D)
16 (F) (G) (H) (J)
17 (A) (B) (C) (D)
18 (F) (G) (H) (J)
19 (A) (B) (C) (D)
20 (F) (G) (H) (J)

21 (A) (B) (C) (D)
22 (F) (G) (H) (J)
23 (A) (B) (C) (D)
24 (F) (G) (H) (J)
25 (A) (B) (C) (D)
26 (F) (G) (H) (J)
27 (A) (B) (C) (D)
28 (F) (G) (H) (J)
29 (A) (B) (C) (D)
30 (F) (G) (H) (J)

Science Standards

Standard 1—Unifying Concepts and Processes *(See page 113.)*
As a result of the activities in grades K–12, all students should develop
understanding and abilities aligned with the following concepts and processes:
- Systems, order, and organization.
- Evidence, models, and explanation.
- Constancy, change, and measurement.
- Evolution and equilibrium.
- Form and function.

Standard 2—Science as Inquiry *(See pages 114–115.)*
As a result of the activities in grades K–4, all students should develop
- The abilities necessary to do scientific inquiry.
- An understanding about scientific inquiry.

Standard 3—Physical Science *(See pages 117–119.)*
As a result of the activities in grades K–4, all students should develop
an understanding of
- Properties of objects and materials.
- Position and motion of objects.
- Light, heat, electricity, and magnetism.

Standard 4—Life Science *(See pages 120–122.)*
As a result of the activities in grades K–4, all students should develop
an understanding of
- Characteristics of organisms.
- Life cycles of organisms.
- Organisms and environments.

Standard 5—Earth and Space Science *(See pages 123–125.)*
As a result of the activities in grades K–4, all students should develop
an understanding of
- Properties of Earth materials.
- Objects in the sky.
- Changes in Earth and sky.

Standard 6—Science and Technology *(See pages 127–128.)*
As a result of the activities in grades K–4, all students should develop
- Abilities to distinguish between natural objects and objects made by humans.
- Abilities of technological design.
- An understanding about science and technology.

Standard 7—Science in Personal and Social Perspectives *(See page 129.)*
As a result of the activities in grades K–4, all students should develop
an understanding of
- Personal health.
- Characteristics and changes in populations.
- Types of resources.
- Changes in environments.
- Science and technology in local challenges.

Science Standards

Standard 8—History and Nature of Science *(See page 130.)*
As a result of the activities in grades K-4, all students should develop an understanding of

• Science as a human endeavor.

Name _____   Date _____

Systems and Models

Unifying Concepts and Processes

DIRECTIONS: Anything with parts that interact, or work together, is called a *system*. On the lines below, write **S** if it is a system and **N** if it is not a system.

Examples:

- A tree is a system because it has roots, a trunk, limbs, and leaves that all work together to help the tree grow.
- A watch is a system because it has parts that work together to keep the correct time.
- A piece of paper is not a system because it does not have any working parts.

_____ 1. television

_____ 2. flower

_____ 3. plastic cup

_____ 4. eraser

_____ 5. automobile

_____ 6. ant

_____ 7. pen

_____ 8. camera

_____ 9. skateboard

_____ 10. towel

_____ 11. balloon

_____ 12. pencil sharpener

Ⓐ

Ⓑ

Ⓒ

Ⓓ

DIRECTIONS: Choose the best answer.

13. In the next column is a series of models that represent the size and placement of the Sun in relation to Earth and the Moon. Which is the best representation of the sun, Earth, and the Moon, overall?

Science Practices

Science as Inquiry

DIRECTIONS: Read about Jeannie's experiment and then answer the questions.

My Question: Is warm water more dense than cold water?

What I Already Know: If two objects take up the same amount of space, the lighter one will be less dense.

What I Did: I filled a beaker with cold water. Then, I filled another beaker with the same amount of warm water. I used red food coloring to color it red. I used an eyedropper to put the warm, red water into the beaker of cold water.

What Happened: The drops of red water floated to the top of the beaker. The red water made a layer on top of the layer of cold water in the beaker.

1. **Jeannie can conclude from her experiment that _____ .**

   Ⓐ warm water is more dense than cold water

   Ⓑ warm water is less dense than cold water

   Ⓒ warm water and cold water have the same density

   Ⓓ neither warm nor cold water have any density

2. **What event does this experiment help Jeannie understand?**

   Ⓕ why it rains in the summer

   Ⓖ why cold water boils so slowly

   Ⓗ why the top layer of the ocean is warmer than the lower layers

   Ⓙ why it is hard to make sugar dissolve in iced tea

DIRECTIONS: Read about Adam's experiment and then answer the questions.

Adam wants to find out how lemon juice reacts when it is combined with different substances. He sets out three paper cups. He puts 1 tablespoon of baking soda in the first cup. He puts 1 tablespoon of salt in the second cup. He puts 1 tablespoon of sugar in the third cup. Then, he puts three drops of lemon juice into each cup. After 30 seconds, he observes all three cups.

3. **What is the variable, or item that changes, in this experiment?**

   Ⓐ the lemon juice

   Ⓑ the amount of time that passed

   Ⓒ the size of the cup

   Ⓓ the type of substance in the cups

4. **What should Adam do if he wants his lab partner to be able to repeat this experiment?**

   Ⓕ Keep accurate records of how he did his experiment and the results.

   Ⓖ Wait until he finishes all the trials before recording any results.

   Ⓗ Estimate the amounts of materials used.

   Ⓘ none of these

5. **What would you expect to happen if Adam repeated this experiment with the cups placed in ice?**

   Ⓐ Any reaction would happen slower.

   Ⓑ The cups would melt.

   Ⓒ Any reaction would happen faster.

   Ⓓ nothing different

Science
2.0

Types of Investigations

Science as Inquiry

DIRECTIONS: For each of the following investigations, write **O** if it would best be accomplished through observation, **C** if it would best be accomplished by collecting specimens, or **E** if it would best be accomplished through doing experiments.

> • When you use **observation,** you are watching what is happening. You are not creating the event.
> • When you **collect specimens,** you are collecting items to be studied.
> • When you **perform an experiment,** you are actively involved in finding an answer to a question, for example, what will happen if you add baking soda to vinegar. Since the baking soda cannot add itself to the vinegar, you must add it. Therefore, you are creating the event.

_____ 1. Determine what items float in water.

_____ 2. Chart the phases of the moon for the month of April.

_____ 3. Determine how a horse's legs move when the horse is trotting.

_____ 4. Categorize the types of rocks that are found in your neighborhood.

_____ 5. Determine what happens when you mix a base and an acid.

_____ 6. Determine how much rainfall is received in a week.

_____ 7. Determine whether the soil in your backyard is the same as that found in a location five miles away.

_____ 8. Determine whether a basketball, baseball, or marble falls more quickly when dropped from the same height.

_____ 9. Determine what microorganisms live in pond water.

_____10. Determine whether a plant will grow in the dark.

_____11. Determine how much a plant grows over a certain period of time.

Science

1.0–2.0

For pages 113–115

Mini-Test 1

Unifying Concepts and Processes; Science as Inquiry

DIRECTIONS: Choose the best answer.

1. **Which of the following is a system?**
   - (A) a beach ball
   - (B) a spoon
   - (C) a CD player
   - (D) a bowl

2. **Which of the following is not a system?**
   - (F) a computer
   - (G) a human hand
   - (H) a rock
   - (J) a lamp

3. **Which of the following shapes would you use to represent the moon in a model?**
   - (A) square
   - (B) circle
   - (C) triangle
   - (D) oval

4. **When keeping records of your observations, it is important that you _____ .**
   - (F) write down everything as it happens
   - (G) change the records to reflect the results you should have gotten
   - (H) record only the results that make sense
   - (J) use red ink

5. **JoLynn and Jon are conducting an experiment. They want to determine how many seconds it takes for a ball to hit the ground when dropped from JoLynn's one-story deck. They take turns dropping the ball and running the stopwatch. When JoLynn drops the ball, Jon records that it takes 3 seconds for it to hit the ground. When Jon drops the ball, JoLynn records that it takes 6 seconds. Why might their results have been different?**
   - (A) They did not drop the ball from the same height.
   - (B) JoLynn started the stopwatch too soon.
   - (C) Jon stopped the stopwatch before the ball hit the ground.
   - (D) all of the above

6. **Which of the following types of investigation would you use to study the courting ritual of the blue heron?**
   - (F) observation
   - (G) collecting specimens
   - (H) doing experiments
   - (J) all of the above

7. **Which of the following types of investigation would you use to determine how fast ice cubes melt under different circumstances?**
   - (A) observation
   - (B) collecting specimens
   - (C) doing experiments
   - (D) all of the above

Science

$\boxed{3.0}$

Heat

Physical Science

DIRECTIONS: Choose the best answer.

1. A log fire represents heat energy produced by _____ .
   - (A) burning
   - (B) friction
   - (C) mixing one thing with another
   - (D) none of the above

2. Rubbing your hands together quickly is an example of heat energy produced by _____ .
   - (F) burning
   - (G) friction
   - (H) mixing one thing with another
   - (J) none of the above

3. An insulated beverage container will _____ .
   - (A) keep hot beverages hot
   - (B) keep cold beverages cold
   - (C) make hot beverages colder
   - (D) both A and B

4. How can you insulate your skin from the cold air when you go outside during the winter months?
   - (F) wear sunscreen
   - (G) wear lotion
   - (H) wear layers of clothing
   - (J) none of the above

5. What is the name of energy from the sun?
   - (A) solar
   - (B) polar
   - (C) nuclear
   - (D) lunar

6. Energy from the sun is transferred to the Earth by _____ .
   - (F) conservation
   - (G) conduction
   - (H) radiation
   - (J) convection

7. Simon left a glass on a windowsill during a sunny day. It had a cube of ice in it. What would you expect to happen over the next hour?
   - (A) The ice cube will melt.
   - (B) The ice cube will evaporate.
   - (C) The ice cube will become larger.
   - (D) none of the above

8. You are sitting outside on a sunny day. What effect will you feel from the sun on your skin?
   - (F) You skin will feel cooler.
   - (G) You skin will feel warmer.
   - (H) You skin will feel softer.
   - (J) You skin will feel the same.

9. You boil a cup of water in the microwave. When you use a thermometer to check the temperature, it reads 100°C. If you leave the water on the counter and check it 30 minutes later, what would you expect the temperature to be?
   - (A) greater than 100°C
   - (B) less than 100°C
   - (C) exactly 100°C
   - (D) 0°C

STOP

Science

3.0

Magnets

Physical Science

DIRECTIONS: Review the list of items below. For each item, write **Y** for *yes* if the item would be attracted to a magnet. Write **N** for *no* if the item would not be attracted to a magnet.

_____ 1. penny

_____ 2. iron needle

_____ 3. rubber band

_____ 4. plastic spoon

_____ 5. steel paper clip

_____ 6. notebook paper

_____ 7. aluminum foil

_____ 8. leather glove

_____ 9. metal screw

_____ 10. cotton ball

_____ 11. nail

_____ 12. ice cube

DIRECTIONS: Choose the best answer.

13. In which direction does a magnetic compass always point?

Ⓐ north

Ⓑ south

Ⓒ east

Ⓓ west

14. What are the north and south ends of a magnet called?

Ⓕ borders

Ⓖ caps

Ⓗ poles

Ⓙ tips

15. Which of the following must occur for two magnets to be attracted to each other?

Ⓐ The north pole of one magnet should be placed next to the north pole of the other magnet.

Ⓑ The south pole of one magnet should be placed next to the south pole of the other magnet.

Ⓒ The north pole of one magnet should be placed next to the south pole of the other magnet.

Ⓓ Magnets are never attracted to one another.

16. What will happen between these two magnets?

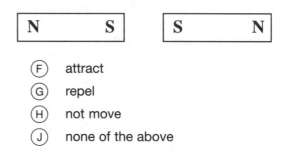

| N | S | | S | N |

Ⓕ attract

Ⓖ repel

Ⓗ not move

Ⓙ none of the above

17. What will happen between these two magnets?

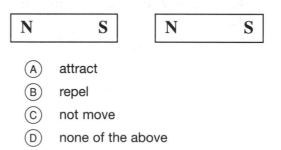

| N | S | | N | S |

Ⓐ attract

Ⓑ repel

Ⓒ not move

Ⓓ none of the above

STOP

Science

3.0

Light

Physical Science

DIRECTIONS: Choose the best answer.

1. A translucent object is one in which
   _____ .

   (A) light can travel through without being changed

   (B) some light can travel through

   (C) no light can travel through

   (D) none of the above

2. An opaque object is one in which _____
   .

   (F) no light can travel through

   (G) light can travel through without being changed

   (H) some light can travel through

   (J) none of the above

3. A transparent object is one in which
   _____ .

   (A) some light can travel through

   (B) no light can travel through

   (C) light can travel through without being changed

   (D) none of the above

4. Which of the following items is translucent?

   (F) cardboard

   (G) tissue paper

   (H) construction paper

   (J) clear glass

5. Which of the following items is opaque?

   (A) tissue paper

   (B) a brick wall

   (C) a window

   (D) eye glasses

6. Which of the following items is transparent?

   (F) eyeglasses

   (G) stained glass

   (H) tin foil

   (J) a brick wall

7. Which of the following has a thick center and thinner edges?

   (A) concave lens

   (B) convex lens

   (C) straight lens

   (D) curved lens

8. Which of the following has a thinner middle than the edges?

   (F) mirror

   (G) prism

   (H) convex lens

   (J) concave lens

9. What tool would you use to split white light into colors?

   (A) a mirror

   (B) a prism

   (C) a convex lens

   (D) a concave lens

10. Which of the following is used in a magnifying glass?

    (F) a prism

    (G) a concave lens

    (H) a mirror

    (J) a convex lens

STOP

Name _____   Date _____

Science

4.0

Characteristics of Organisms

Life Science

DIRECTIONS: Choose the best answer.

> Organisms have basic needs. Animals need air, water, and food. Plants need air, water, nutrients, and light. Organisms can survive only in environments in which their needs can be met.
>
> Each plant or animal has different structures that serve different functions in growth, survival, and reproduction. For example, humans have fingers to grasp objects.

1. **What do flowers use to absorb sunlight?**
   - (A) leaves
   - (B) roots
   - (C) stems
   - (D) petals

2. **What do fish use to breathe?**
   - (F) fins
   - (G) scales
   - (H) gills
   - (J) lungs

3. **What part of a tree absorbs nutrients and water?**
   - (A) the leaves
   - (B) the roots
   - (C) the trunk
   - (D) the branches

4. **Which of the following would you find living in the desert?**
   - (F) duck
   - (G) cactus
   - (H) trout
   - (J) water lily

5. **Which of the following would you not find living in a swamp?**
   - (A) frog
   - (B) turtle
   - (C) alligator
   - (D) dolphin

6. **Which of the following would you not find living in a meadow?**
   - (F) sunflower
   - (G) mouse
   - (H) grasshopper
   - (J) shark

7. **One similarity between a lion cub and a flower seedling is that _____ .**
   - (A) they both need water to survive
   - (B) they are both cared for by their parents
   - (C) they both eat the same kinds of food
   - (D) all of the above are true

8. **One difference between a lion cub and a flower seedling is that only the _____ .**
   - (F) lion cub needs food
   - (G) flower seedling needs water
   - (H) lion cub can move from place to place
   - (J) flower seedling has parents

Name _____ Date _____

Science

4.0

Life Cycles of Plants and Animals

Life Science

DIRECTIONS: Number each stage of the life cycle in the order it occurs.

1. Moth

_____ larva

_____ adult moth

_____ egg

_____ pupa

2. Oak Tree

_____ tree

_____ acorn

_____ seedling

3. Pig

_____ newborn

_____ piglet

_____ adult pig

4. Adult

_____ child

_____ adult

_____ newborn

_____ adolescent

5. Frog

_____ adult frog

_____ tadpole

_____ egg

DIRECTIONS: Read the following passage. Then, answer the questions.

Butterfly Life Cycle

The life of a butterfly begins when an adult female butterfly lays an egg on a plant. It usually takes two to three weeks for the embryo to grow in the egg. The egg then hatches into a caterpillar. The caterpillar eats a large amount of food and grows. In about two to three months, it will attach itself to a twig. It forms a hard outer shell called a *chrysalis*, or pupa. The caterpillar now changes or matures into a butterfly. It normally takes about two weeks before a full-grown adult butterfly appears. It will then fly away to look for a partner, mate, and reproduce, starting the cycle all over again.

6. The hard outer shell in which a caterpillar transforms into a butterfly is called a(n) _____ .

(A) casing

(B) egg

(C) chrysalis

(D) none of the above

7. Which stage of a butterfly's life follows the egg stage?

(F) caterpillar

(G) chrysalis

(H) juvenile

(J) adult

8. Once in the chrysalis, how long does it typically take for a caterpillar to change into a butterfly?

(A) one day

(B) one week

(C) ten days

(D) two weeks

STOP

Science
4.0

Adaptive Characteristics

Life Science

DIRECTIONS: Match the ecosystem of each mystery organism in **Column A** to one or more adaptations that would be most beneficial for its survival in **Column B.**

Column A

1. _____ in a tree in the rain forest

2. _____ underground in the backyard

3. _____ on the leaves of a rose bush

4. _____ in a coral reef

5. _____ on a glacier in Alaska

6. _____ on a mountainside

7. _____ in a polluted stream

8. _____ in the desert

9. _____ on the side of a cliff

10. _____ in a cave

11. _____ in a forest in the midwest

12. _____ on the bank of a nearly dry stream

Column B

A. strong legs for climbing

B. a tail to help it hang from branches

C. deep roots to find water

D. the ability to breathe air as well as water

E. being a color that blends in with leaves

F. strong claws for digging and moving dirt

G. a thick coat and layer of fat

H. strong wings to fly and glide

I. ability to see in the dark

J. clear eyelids to keep out sand and dirt

K. hibernating in the winter when food is scarce

L. ability to completely draw inside a shell

Science

5.0

Rocks and Minerals

Earth and Space Science

DIRECTIONS: Choose the best answer.

1. **Which of the following statements is true?**

    (A) All rocks are minerals, but not all minerals are rocks.

    (B) All minerals are rocks, but not all rocks are minerals.

    (C) There is no relationship between rocks and minerals.

    (D) Rocks and minerals are two different words for the same thing.

2. **Obsidian, a mineral that is also known as *volcanic glass*, is _____ .**

    (F) soft and shiny

    (G) hard and shiny

    (H) hard and rough

    (J) soft and rough

3. **Which of the following rocks is light, has a rough texture, and has many hollow spaces?**

    (A) granite

    (B) shale

    (C) graphite

    (D) pumice

4. **Which of the following rocks is the texture of sandpaper?**

    (F) granite

    (G) shale

    (H) sandstone

    (J) marble

5. **A rock leaves a white streak when it is scraped across a surface. It probably contains which mineral that is used to make powder?**

    (A) gold

    (B) iron

    (C) talc

    (D) graphite

6. **Which type of rock splits apart in layers, is usually gray or black, and is often used to make blackboards?**

    (F) slate

    (G) marble

    (H) sandstone

    (J) granite

7. **Which of the following minerals is the hardest?**

    (A) talc

    (B) gold

    (C) iron

    (D) diamond

8. **When a mineral breaks with rough edges, it is said to have the property of _____ .**

    (F) luster

    (G) streak

    (H) fracture

    (J) cleavage

9. **Which of the following would not help you identify a mineral?**

    (A) tendency to float

    (B) hardness

    (C) streak

    (D) cleavage

Science
5.0

Weathering and Erosion

Earth and Space Science

DIRECTIONS: Read the definitions in the chart below. Use the chart to help you answer the questions.

Term	What is it?
Weathering	The process that wears down rocks. Wind, water, ice, and chemicals all cause weathering. Weathering changes the shapes or forms of rocks.
Erosion	The process that moves rocks. Wind, moving water, and the movement of glaciers can all cause erosion.
Sediment	Rock, sand, or dirt that has been carried to another place by wind, water, or a glacier.
Glacier	A large body of ice that slowly moves across land. As it moves, it pushes sand and rock and carries them to other places.
Soil	Dirt or earth that is made up of weathered rocks.

1. **Which of the following forces does not cause weathering?**

   (A) wind

   (B) water

   (C) chemicals

   (D) friction

2. **Which of the following is the process that moves rocks by wind, water, or glaciers?**

   (F) weathering

   (G) erosion

   (H) sediment

   (J) soil

3. **What is the term for dirt or earth that is made up of weathered rocks?**

   (A) sediment

   (B) silt

   (C) soil

   (D) glacier

4. **Which of the following statements about weathering is not true?**

   (F) It wears down rocks.

   (G) It moves rocks to other places.

   (H) It changes the shapes of rocks.

   (J) It can be caused by chemicals.

5. **Look at the two pictures below. The changes to the shoreline are most likely due to**

   _____ .

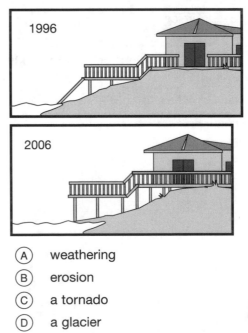

   (A) weathering

   (B) erosion

   (C) a tornado

   (D) a glacier

Name _____ Date _____

Science
5.0

Planets in the Solar System

Earth and Space Science

DIRECTIONS: Fill in the blanks with the names of planets according to their correct order from the sun.

1. _____

2. _____

3. _____

4. _____

5. _____

6. _____

7. _____

8. _____

9. _____

STOP

Science

3.0–5.0

For pages 117–125

Mini-Test 2

Physical Science; Life Science; Earth and Space Science

DIRECTIONS: Choose the best answer.

1. **Which of the following is a way to produce heat energy?**

    (A) by burning

    (B) by friction

    (C) by mixing one thing with another

    (D) all of the above

2. **The temperature of a cup of water taken from the refrigerator is recorded at 38°F. After sitting on the counter for 30 minutes, the temperature is recorded at 62°F. What has happened?**

    (F) The water has gotten colder.

    (G) The water has gotten warmer.

    (H) There is no change in the water.

    (J) The water has evaporated.

3. **Why would a nail be attracted to a magnet?**

    (A) It is made of steel or iron.

    (B) It weighs less than the magnet.

    (C) It is thinner than the magnet.

    (D) all of the above

4. **Which of the following items is transparent?**

    (F) rock

    (G) lamp shade

    (H) clear glass jar

    (J) piece of wood

5. **Which animal would not be found in a pond ecosystem?**

    (A) rabbit

    (B) insect

    (C) fish

    (D) frog

6. **A caterpillar is one stage in the life cycle of a _____ .**

    (F) praying mantis

    (G) butterfly

    (H) honeybee

    (J) cicada

7. **An adaptation related to a fox's keen sense of hearing is the fox's _____ .**

    (A) long, bushy tail

    (B) long snout

    (C) large, upright ears

    (D) sharp, canine teeth

8. **All _____ are _____ .**

    (F) minerals, rock

    (G) rocks, fossils

    (H) rocks, minerals

    (J) fossils, minerals

9. **What forces cause erosion?**

    (A) water, gravity, and Sun

    (B) Sun, wind, and glaciers

    (C) wind, water, and glaciers

    (D) gravity, wind, and Sun

10. **What is the largest planet in our solar system?**

    (F) Earth

    (G) Neptune

    (H) Jupiter

    (J) Saturn

Science

6.0

Tools Used in Science

Science and Technology

DIRECTIONS: Choose the best answer.

1. **Which of the following would you use to measure the speed of a falling object?**
   - (A) a stopwatch
   - (B) a microscope
   - (C) a balance scale
   - (D) a ruler

2. **Which of the following would be used to look more closely at a leaf?**
   - (F) a beaker
   - (G) a magnifying glass
   - (H) a barometer
   - (J) binoculars

3. **Which of the following would you use to study cells?**
   - (A) a telescope
   - (B) a magnifying glass
   - (C) a microscope
   - (D) binoculars

4. **Which of the following would you use to determine the boiling point of a liquid?**
   - (F) a barometer
   - (G) a thermometer
   - (H) a ruler
   - (J) a scale

5. **Which of the following would you use to study the stars?**
   - (A) a magnifying glass
   - (B) a microscope
   - (C) binoculars
   - (D) a telescope

6. **Which of the following would you use to determine which of two objects is heavier?**
   - (F) a ruler
   - (G) a balance scale
   - (H) a barometer
   - (J) a beaker

7. **Which of the following would you use to measure the height of a plant?**
   - (A) a microscope
   - (B) a ruler
   - (C) a barometer
   - (D) a scale

8. **Which of the following would you use to determine the outside temperature?**
   - (F) a thermometer
   - (G) a barometer
   - (H) a measuring stick
   - (J) a rain gauge

9. **Which of the following would you use to determine the weight of a rock?**
   - (A) a beaker
   - (B) a stopwatch
   - (C) a scale
   - (D) a ruler

10. **Which of the following would you need to measure a liquid for an experiment?**
    - (F) a rain gauge
    - (G) a telescope
    - (H) a beaker
    - (J) a thermometer

STOP

Name _____   Date _____

Distinguishing Between
Natural and Human-Made Objects

Science and Technology

DIRECTIONS: For each of the following, write **N** if it is a natural object or **H** if it is a human-made object.

Clue   **Natural objects** are ones that exist in nature. **Human-made objects** are ones that have been designed and made by people.

1. _____   2. _____   3. _____   4. _____

5. _____   6. _____   7. _____   8. _____

9. _____   10. _____   11. _____   12. _____

STOP

Science

| 7.0 |

Personal Health and Safety

Science in Personal and Social Perspectives

DIRECTIONS: Choose the best answer.

1. **What is the best way to avoid catching a cold?**

   - Ⓐ Wash your hands regularly.
   - Ⓑ Cover your mouth when sneezing.
   - Ⓒ Dress warmly.
   - Ⓓ Brush your teeth regularly.

2. **Which of the following is a problem caused by smoking?**

   - Ⓕ bad breath
   - Ⓖ yellow teeth
   - Ⓗ smelly clothing
   - Ⓙ all of the above

3. **How often should you visit the dentist?**

   - Ⓐ once a year
   - Ⓑ twice a year
   - Ⓒ once a month
   - Ⓓ once every two years

4. **Which of the following drinks contains the most sugar?**

   - Ⓕ milk
   - Ⓖ water
   - Ⓗ diet soda
   - Ⓙ orange juice

5. **Which of the following is a healthy snack?**

   - Ⓐ ice cream
   - Ⓑ chocolate chip cookies
   - Ⓒ grapes
   - Ⓓ chips

6. **Approximately how much sleep should a third-grader get each night?**

   - Ⓕ 6 hours
   - Ⓖ 8 hours
   - Ⓗ 10 hours
   - Ⓙ 12 hours

7. **Which of the following is a benefit of exercise?**

   - Ⓐ It makes your muscles stronger.
   - Ⓑ It strengthens your bones.
   - Ⓒ It helps you avoid gaining weight.
   - Ⓓ all of the above

8. **If a stranger approaches you and asks you for help, you should _____ .**

   - Ⓕ run or walk the other way
   - Ⓖ yell for help if you feel you are in danger
   - Ⓗ stay out of the stranger's car
   - Ⓙ all of the above

9. **Which of the following should you do when riding a bicycle?**

   - Ⓐ wear a bike helmet
   - Ⓑ ride barefoot
   - Ⓒ listen to loud music through headphones
   - Ⓓ avoid using the handlebars

10. **What is the first thing you should do if there is a fire in your house?**

    - Ⓕ call 911
    - Ⓖ hide under your bed or other furniture
    - Ⓗ try to get outside quickly and safely
    - Ⓙ go to the highest point in the house

Science
8.0

Types of Scientists

History and Nature of Science

DIRECTIONS: Choose the best answer.

1. A person who studies the history of the earth, especially as recorded in rocks, is a _____ .
   - (A) physicist
   - (B) geologist
   - (C) biologist
   - (D) chemist

2. A person who studies stars, planets, and galaxies is a(n) _____ .
   - (F) astronomer
   - (G) meteorologist
   - (H) geologist
   - (J) archaeologist

3. A person who studies matter, energy, and how they are related is a(n) _____ .
   - (A) chemist
   - (B) biologist
   - (C) physicist
   - (D) astronomer

4. A person who studies weather and climate is a(n) _____ .
   - (F) physicist
   - (G) astronomer
   - (H) meteorologist
   - (J) biologist

5. A person who studies living things is a(n) _____ .
   - (A) astronomer
   - (B) chemist
   - (C) biologist
   - (D) physicist

6. A person who studies the ocean is a(n) _____ .
   - (F) astronomer
   - (G) oceanographer
   - (H) meteorologist
   - (J) ecologist

7. A person who mixes different substances together to create new things is a _____ .
   - (A) chemist
   - (B) biologist
   - (C) physicist
   - (D) geologist

8. A person who studies the relationships between organisms and their environment is a(n) _____ .
   - (F) chemist
   - (G) ecologist
   - (H) geologist
   - (J) astronomer

9. A person who studies the human heart is a _____ .
   - (A) cardiologist
   - (B) chemist
   - (C) biologist
   - (D) geologist

10. A person who studies skin diseases is a(n) _____ .
    - (F) physicist
    - (G) biologist
    - (H) dermatologist
    - (J) astronomer

STOP

Science

| 6.0–8.0 |

For pages 127–130

Mini-Test 3

Science and Technology; Science in Personal and Social
Perspectives; History and Nature of Science

DIRECTIONS: Choose the best answer.

1. **Which of the following tools would you use to study Saturn?**
   - (A) a microscope
   - (B) a telescope
   - (C) a magnifying glass
   - (D) binoculars

2. **Which of the following tools would you use to study a strand of human hair?**
   - (F) a beaker
   - (G) a telescope
   - (H) a microscope
   - (J) a barometer

3. **Objects that exist in nature are called _____ objects.**
   - (A) life-like
   - (B) natural
   - (C) human-made
   - (D) normal

4. **Which of the following objects is a natural object?**
   - (F) flower
   - (G) gate
   - (H) car
   - (J) baseball

5. **Which of the following objects is a human-made object?**
   - (A) star
   - (B) tadpole
   - (C) telephone
   - (D) rock

6. **Which of the following is an unhealthy snack?**
   - (F) an apple
   - (G) tuna salad
   - (H) chocolate pudding
   - (J) an orange

7. **What should you do to help prevent the spread of germs when coughing?**
   - (A) Cover your mouth with your hand.
   - (B) Cover your mouth with a tissue.
   - (C) Lower your head when coughing.
   - (D) Cough without covering your mouth.

8. **A meteorologist is a person who studies _____ .**
   - (F) rocks
   - (G) living things
   - (H) weather
   - (J) plants

9. **An astronomer is a person who studies _____ .**
   - (A) animals
   - (B) the weather
   - (C) stars
   - (D) water

10. **A biologist is a person who studies _____ .**
   - (F) fossils
   - (G) living things
   - (H) rocks
   - (J) energy

STOP

How Am I Doing?

Mini-Test 1 Page 116 **Number Correct** [ ]	**7** answers correct	**Great Job!** Move on to the section test on page 133.
	5–6 answers correct	**You're almost there!** But you still need a little practice. Review practice pages 113–115 before moving on to the section test on page 133.
	0–4 answers correct	**Oops!** Time to review what you have learned and try again. Review the practice section on pages 113–115. Then, retake the test on page 116. Now, move on to the section test on page 133.
Mini-Test 2 Page 126 **Number Correct** [ ]	**10** answers correct	**Awesome!** Move on to the section test on page 133.
	6–9 answers correct	**You're almost there!** But you still need a little practice. Review practice pages 117–125 before moving on to the section test on page 133.
	0–5 answers correct	**Oops!** Time to review what you have learned and try again. Review the practice section on pages 117–125. Then, retake the test on page 126. Now, move on to the section test on page 133.
Mini-Test 3 Page 131 **Number Correct** [ ]	**10** answers correct	**Great Job!** Move on to the section test on page 133.
	6–9 answers correct	**You're almost there!** But you still need a little practice. Review practice pages 127–130 before moving on to the section test on page 133.
	0–5 answers correct	**Oops!** Time to review what you have learned and try again. Review the practice section on pages 127–130. Then, retake the test on page 131. Now, move on to the section test on page 133.

Name _____ Date _____

Final Science Test
for pages 113–131

DIRECTIONS: Choose the best answer.

1. **How does a keyboard interact with the computer system?**
   - (A) It allows data to be printed.
   - (B) It allows data to be viewed.
   - (C) It allows data to be input.
   - (D) It allows data to be stored.

2. **Which of the following shapes would you use to represent a chicken egg if you were creating a model?**
   - (F) rectangle
   - (G) oval
   - (H) circle
   - (J) square

3. **Why should you keep a record of an investigation?**
   - (A) so you can see exactly what was done during the investigation
   - (B) so others can repeat the investigation
   - (C) both A and B
   - (D) neither A nor B

4. **When should observations be recorded?**
   - (F) at the time of the observation
   - (G) within a day of the observation
   - (H) a week following the observation
   - (J) There is no reason to record observations.

5. **Which of the following types of investigation would you use to determine what happens when water and vinegar are mixed?**
   - (A) observation
   - (B) collecting specimens
   - (C) experimentation
   - (D) all of the above

6. **Which of the following activities does not produce heat energy?**
   - (F) rubbing your hands together briskly
   - (G) using sandpaper to sand wood
   - (H) burning coal
   - (J) sitting in the sun

7. **An item that prevents the transfer of heat has which property?**
   - (A) insulation
   - (B) radiation
   - (C) friction
   - (D) refrigeration

8. **What will happen to hot soup that is put into a thermos?**
   - (F) It will become hotter.
   - (G) It will stay warm.
   - (H) It will cool quickly.
   - (J) It will become icy.

9. **The temperature of a glass of water sitting on your kitchen counter is 68°F, the same as the temperature in the room. What will be the temperature of the water when you measure it an hour later?**
   - (A) It will be warmer than room temperature.
   - (B) It will be colder than room temperature.
   - (C) It will be the same as room temperature.
   - (D) There is no way to predict this.

10. **A magnet cannot move which of the following objects?**
    - (F) a paper clip
    - (G) a nail
    - (H) a toothpick
    - (J) a staple

11. **Magdalena has dropped a box of antique needles into a haystack. Some of the needles are made of wood, some are made of iron, and some are made of bone. If she runs a magnet over the haystack, which needles will she be able to find?**

- (A) the wooden needles
- (B) the iron needles
- (C) the bone needles
- (D) none of the needles

12. **What will happen if the north pole of one magnet is placed near the south pole of a second magnet?**

- (F) The magnets will attract.
- (G) The magnets will repel.
- (H) The magnets will not move.
- (J) none of the above

13. **You have a frosted glass shower door installed in your bathroom. Which of the following terms would you use to describe the door?**

- (A) opaque
- (B) translucent
- (C) transparent
- (D) obscure

14. **A prism is a tool that _____ .**

- (F) magnifies objects
- (G) lets you see things that are far away
- (H) has a thick center and thin edges
- (J) splits white light into colors

15. **Which of the following would you not find living in a forest?**

- (A) raccoon
- (B) alligator
- (C) deer
- (D) poison ivy

16. **Which of the following is the second stage in the life cycle of an eagle?**

- (F) fledgling
- (G) adult eagle
- (H) hatchling
- (J) egg

17. **What is an adaptation?**

- (A) a trait or ability that helps an organism survive in its environment
- (B) the number of pairs of genes a particular organism has
- (C) the ways in which an organism can travel
- (D) an organism's place in the food chain

18. **An example of an adaptation would be _____ .**

- (F) a dog shedding its heavy coat in the summer
- (G) the thorns on a rose bush
- (H) a tiger's sharp teeth and claws
- (J) all of the above

19. **Which of the following is the name for volcanic glass?**

- (A) gold
- (B) sandstone
- (C) obsidian
- (D) quartz

20. **Which of the following tests can help you to identify a mineral?**

- (F) hardness
- (G) luster
- (H) cleavage
- (J) all of the above

GO

21. Which of the following minerals is the softest?

(A) diamond

(B) gypsum

(C) quartz

(D) silver

22. Two forces that cause erosion are water and _____ .

(F) Sun

(G) wind

(H) gravity

(J) friction

23. Which planet in our solar system is closest to the sun?

(A) Pluto

(B) Mars

(C) Mercury

(D) Saturn

24. Which of the following tools would you use to watch birds hatching in a nest in your backyard?

(F) a microscope

(G) a telescope

(H) a magnifying glass

(J) binoculars

25. Which of the following tools would you use to measure how far a ball rolled?

(A) a stopwatch

(B) a measuring tape

(C) a barometer

(D) a scale

26. Which of the following objects is not a natural object?

(F) the moon

(G) a volcano

(H) an anteater

(J) a rake

27. What can you do to prevent getting a sunburn?

(A) wear long sleeves

(B) wear sunscreen

(C) wear a wide-brimmed hat

(D) all of the above

28. An astronomer is a person who studies _____ .

(F) remains of past civilizations

(G) living things

(H) stars and planets

(J) rocks

29. A geologist is a person who studies _____ .

(A) water

(B) weather and climate

(C) rocks

(D) meteors

STOP

Final Science Test

Answer Sheet

1 Ⓐ Ⓑ Ⓒ Ⓓ
2 Ⓕ Ⓖ Ⓗ Ⓙ
3 Ⓐ Ⓑ Ⓒ Ⓓ
4 Ⓕ Ⓖ Ⓗ Ⓙ
5 Ⓐ Ⓑ Ⓒ Ⓓ
6 Ⓕ Ⓖ Ⓗ Ⓙ
7 Ⓐ Ⓑ Ⓒ Ⓓ
8 Ⓕ Ⓖ Ⓗ Ⓙ
9 Ⓐ Ⓑ Ⓒ Ⓓ
10 Ⓕ Ⓖ Ⓗ Ⓙ

11 Ⓐ Ⓑ Ⓒ Ⓓ
12 Ⓕ Ⓖ Ⓗ Ⓙ
13 Ⓐ Ⓑ Ⓒ Ⓓ
14 Ⓕ Ⓖ Ⓗ Ⓙ
15 Ⓐ Ⓑ Ⓒ Ⓓ
16 Ⓕ Ⓖ Ⓗ Ⓙ
17 Ⓐ Ⓑ Ⓒ Ⓓ
18 Ⓕ Ⓖ Ⓗ Ⓙ
19 Ⓐ Ⓑ Ⓒ Ⓓ
20 Ⓕ Ⓖ Ⓗ Ⓙ

21 Ⓐ Ⓑ Ⓒ Ⓓ
22 Ⓕ Ⓖ Ⓗ Ⓙ
23 Ⓐ Ⓑ Ⓒ Ⓓ
24 Ⓕ Ⓖ Ⓗ Ⓙ
25 Ⓐ Ⓑ Ⓒ Ⓓ
26 Ⓕ Ⓖ Ⓗ Ⓙ
27 Ⓐ Ⓑ Ⓒ Ⓓ
28 Ⓕ Ⓖ Ⓗ Ⓙ
29 Ⓐ Ⓑ Ⓒ Ⓓ

Answer Key

Page 9
1. A
2. H

Page 10
1. B
2. F
3. A
4. J

Page 11
1. D
2. G
3. B
4. G

Pages 12–13
1. B
2. H
3. A
4. J
5. Answers will vary. Students should explain which genre they prefer and give reasons for their answer.

Page 14
1. A. His father has a great name.
B. His grandfather won the cup, or horse race, at Newmarket two years in a row.
C. His grandmother had a sweet temper, or personality.
D. His mother never kicks or bites.
2. having a proud family history; being gentle and good
3. F

Page 15
1. A
2. J
3. A
4. H
5. B
6. J
7. C
8. J

Page 16
1. C
2. J
3. C
4. G
5. B
6. J
7. D

Page 17
1. C
2. J
3. A
4. F

Page 18
Mini-Test 1
1. D
2. G
3. C
4. J
5. A
6. G

Page 19
1. C
2. J
3. B
4. H
5. C
6. G
7. A

Page 20
1. Ms. Warner; she asked Jason what was wrong and made a phone call.
2. Jason; he forgot his lunch.

3. Jason's mother; she brought Jason's lunch to school.
4. All three passages describe the morning that Jason forgot to bring his lunch to school.

Page 21
1. The main characters are Juan and Bill.
2. The story takes place at Juan's house.
3. The story takes place in the present.
4. Juan is nervous because he has not seen his friend Bill for six months. He's not sure if they will still feel like good friends.
5. Some clues in the story that helped show that Juan is nervous: he keeps checking the clock, he paces the floor, and he wonders if they are still friends.
6. Juan tries to act calm and pretends that Bill never moved away.

Page 22
1. Students should state their favorite class.
2. Students should explain why the class they chose is their favorite.

3. Answers will vary. Students' poems, stories, or letters should describe their ideas and feelings about their favorite class. Their writings should be appropriate for their audience.

Page 23
Students' paragraphs should have a main idea, supporting details, and a conclusion.

Page 24
1. A
2. J
3. warm, winter. Details: Ants dig into the ground. Female grasshoppers lay their eggs and die. Bees gather in the middle of their hive.

Page 25
1. Answers will vary. Students should write a paragraph that describes how to make or do something. They should include transitional words between each step of the process.
2. Answers will vary. Students should write the same procedure using numbered steps.

Page 26
1. D
2. G
3. B
4. H
5. C
6. J
7. C
8. F
9. D
10. H
11. C

Page 27
1. C
2. J
3. A
4. G
5. D
6. F
7. C
8. J
9. A

Page 28
1. D
2. H
3. B
4. G
5. C
6. J
7. A
8. H
9. C

Page 29
Mini-Test 2
1. B
2. She says "from her father and me."
3. G
4. A
5. H
6. C
7. H
8. D

Page 30
Students should enter the main topic in the center circle. Ideas about the main topic should connect to the center circle. Further breakdown of these ideas should be connected to the appropriate idea.

Pages 31–32
1. B
2. C
3. A
4. D
5. C
6. D
7. B
8. A
9. D
10. C
11. B
12. B
13. J
14. B
15. H
16. C
17. J
18. C
19. G
20. C

Page 33
Mini-Test 3
1. D
2. H
3. A
4. G
5. D
6. F
7. C
8. J
9. C
10. H

Page 34
1. how the Sun and the Moon came to live in the sky
2. how the Moon and the stars came into existence
3. Both stories discuss how items in the sky came to be there.

Page 35
1. Students should describe their main characters.
2. Students should discuss where and when their stories take place.
3. Students should present the main problems that will be introduced in their stories and how they will be resolved by the main characters.
4. Students should explain how they want readers to react to their stories.
5. Students should have another person read and critique their stories.

Page 36
Letters should explain why the student should be allowed to do something of his or her choosing. Students should construct their letters with an appropriate greeting and closing and use correct punctuation and spelling.

Page 37 Mini-Test 4
1. B
2. G
3. Students should write a thank-you note to someone who has given them a gift or done something for them.

Pages 40–42 Final English Language Arts Test
1. C
2. G
3. B
4. H
5. B
6. G
7. A
8. F
9. B
10. H
11. D
12. J
13. D
14. H
15. A
16. J
17. C
18. J
19. C
20. J
21. D
22. F

Page 45
1. C
2. G
3. D
4. G
5. B
6. H
7. C
8. H
9. C

Page 46
1. B
2. J
3. D
4. G
5. B
6. J
7. D
8. F

Page 47
1. C
2. F
3. D
4. J
5. B
6. G
7. C
8. F
9. C
10. G

Page 48
1. B
2. F
3. A
4. H
5. D
6. F
7. C
8. H
9. A
10. G

Mini-Test 1
1. C
2. H
3. B
4. F
5. D
6. F
7. C

Page 117
1. A
2. G
3. D
4. H
5. A
6. H
7. A
8. G
9. B

Page 118
1. N
2. Y
3. N
4. N
5. Y
6. N
7. N
8. N
9. Y
10. N
11. Y
12. N
13. A
14. H
15. C
16. G
17. A

Page 119
1. B
2. F
3. C
4. G
5. B
6. F
7. B
8. J
9. B
10. J

Page 120
1. A
2. H
3. B
4. G
5. D
6. J
7. A
8. H

Page 121
1. 2, 4, 1, 3
2. 3, 1, 2
3. 1, 2, 3
4. 2, 4, 1, 3
5. 3, 2, 1
6. C
7. F
8. D

Page 122
1. B
2. F
3. E
4. L
5. G
6. A
7. D
8. J
9. H
10. I
11. K
12. C

Page 123
1. A
2. G
3. D
4. H
5. C
6. F
7. D
8. H
9. A

Page 124
1. D
2. G
3. C
4. G
5. B

Page 125
1. Mercury
2. Venus
3. Earth
4. Mars
5. Jupiter
6. Saturn
7. Uranus
8. Neptune
9. Pluto

Page 126
Mini-Test 2
1. D
2. G
3. A
4. H
5. A
6. G
7. C
8. H
9. C
10. H

Page 127
1. A
2. G
3. C
4. G
5. D
6. G
7. B
8. F
9. C
10. H

Page 128
1. N
2. N
3. H
4. H
5. N
6. H
7. N
8. H
9. N
10. N
11. H
12. N

Page 129
1. A
2. J
3. B
4. J
5. C
6. H
7. D
8. J
9. A
10. H

Page 130
1. B
2. F
3. C
4. H
5. C
6. G
7. A
8. G
9. A
10. H

Page 131
Mini-Test 3
1. B
2. H
3. B
4. F
5. C
6. H
7. B
8. H
9. C
10. H

Pages 133–135
Final Science Test
1. C
2. G
3. C
4. F
5. C
6. J
7. A
8. G
9. C
10. H
11. B
12. F
13. B
14. J
15. B
16. H
17. A
18. J
19. C
20. J
21. B
22. G
23. C
24. J
25. B
26. J
27. D
28. H
29. C

Page 49
1. C
2. G
3. C
4. G
5. D
6. G

Page 50
1. B
2. F
3. B
4. H
5. C
6. G

Page 51
1. B
2. H
3. D
4. H
5. A
6. J
7. C
8. G
9. A

Page 52
1. 12, 27, 13, 45;
   Rule: subtract 10
2. 90, 46, 25, 42
   Rule: add 9
3. 15, 17, 50, 30;
   Rule: divide by 2

Page 53
1.

2.

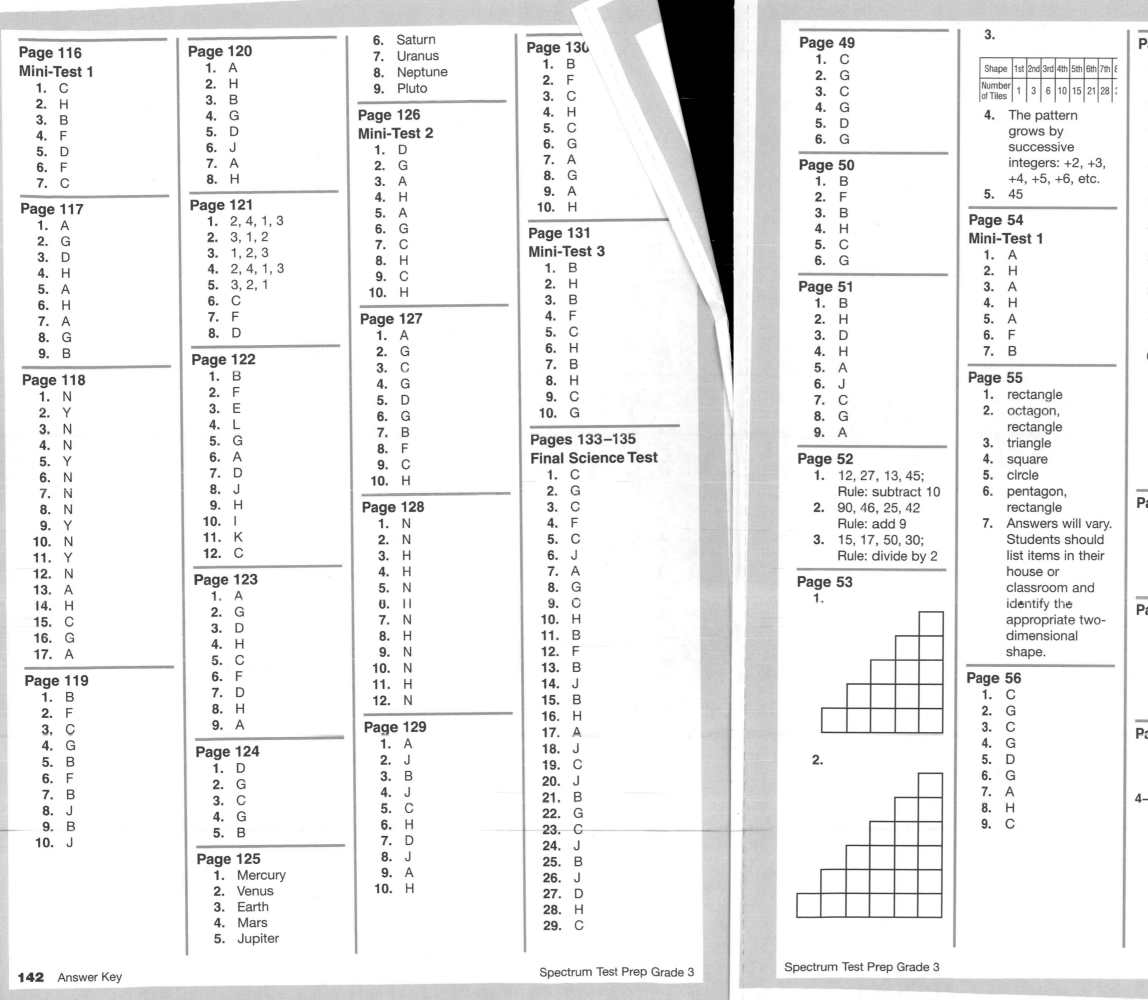

3.

Shape	1st	2nd	3rd	4th	5th	6th	7th	8
Number of Tiles	1	3	6	10	15	21	28	

4. The pattern grows by successive integers: +2, +3, +4, +5, +6, etc.
5. 45

Page 54
Mini-Test 1
1. A
2. H
3. A
4. H
5. A
6. F
7. B

Page 55
1. rectangle
2. octagon, rectangle
3. triangle
4. square
5. circle
6. pentagon, rectangle
7. Answers will vary. Students should list items in their house or classroom and identify the appropriate two-dimensional shape.

Page 56
1. C
2. G
3. C
4. G
5. D
6. G
7. A
8. H
9. C

Page 57

1. Answers will vary. Check coordinates for accuracy.
2. Answers will vary. Check coordinates for accuracy.

Page 58
1. C
2. J
3. C
4. G
5. D

Page 59
1. rotation
2. reflection
3. reflection
4. rotation
5. rotation
6. reflection

Page 60
1. C
2. J
3. C
4–6. Students' drawings of real-life objects will vary. The objects should be based on the shape that was described.

Page 61
1. C
2. J
3. B

Page 62
1. 21
2. 2
3. 2
4. 52,800
5. 5
6. 10
7. 62
8. 36
9. 340 mm
10. yes
11. 300 cm
12. no
13. 1,000 cm × 1,200 cm

Page 63
1. A
2. J
3. A
4. G
5. A
6. G
7. C

Page 64
1. B
2. H
3. D
4. J
5. B
6. F

Page 65
Mini-Test 2
1. B
2. G
3. D
4. F
5. C
6. J
7. C
8. F

Pages 66–67
1. D
2. H
3. 5, 13, 8, 6, 2
4. bar for size 6 to 13;
   bar for size 7 to 8;
   bar for size 8 to 6
5. B
6. F
7. B
8. G

Page 68
1. A
2. J
3. C
4. J
5. D
6. G
7. C

Page 69
1. B
2. F
3. C
4. G
5. D
6. H
7. A
8. H

Page 70
1. B
2. G
3. A
4. F
5. A
6. J
7. A

Page 71
1. B
2. H
3. D
4. G
5. C
6. F
7. A
8. F

Page 72
1. C
2. F
3. D
4. J
5. D

Page 73
Mini-Test 3
1. C
2. H
3. C
4. F
5. C
6. F
7. A

Pages 75–77 Final Mathematics Test
1. A
2. H
3. D
4. H
5. A
6. H
7. C
8. G
9. C
10. H
11. A
12. H
13. D
14. G
15. B
16. F
17. D
18. G
19. A
20. G
21. D
22. F
23. D

Page 80
1. C
2. F
3. B
4. G

Page 81
1. A
2. H
3. B
4. J

Page 82
1. B
2. F
3. B
4. F
5. C
6. G

Page 83
1. B
2. H
3. A
4. H
5. Answers will vary. Students may mention the length of travel, the long days, having to walk much of the way, or using oxen to pull the wagon.

Page 84
1. G
2. E
3. B
4. A
5. F
6. C
7. D

Page 85
1. D
2. H
3. B
4. F

Page 86
1. L
2. E
3. B
4. G
5. C
6. H
7. I
8. F
9. D
10. K
11. A
12. J

Page 87
Mini-Test 1
1. B
2. J
3. A
4. G
5. D
6. J
7. B
8. F

Page 88
Students should describe a change in their life, such as a new interest or skill, or a new home or school. They should describe how this change has affected their lives.

Page 89
Students should describe one of their family traditions.

Page 90
Answers will vary. Students should list two groups of which they are members. They should then list some of their roles/behaviors in these groups. For example, as a student in their class at school, they might list such responsibilities as paying attention in class, participating in class discussions, and completing homework assignments. As a member of a sports team, they might mention being on time for practices and games, and following the coach's directions.

Page 91
1. B
2. H
3. A
4. G
5. A

6. J
7. B
8. F

Page 92
Mini-Test 2
1. A
2. G
3. D
4. G
5. B
6. J
7. C
8. J
9. A

Page 93
1. B
2. G
3. A
4. G
5. B
6. G
7. B
8. G
9. B
10. F

Page 94
1. D
2. H
3. B
4. G
5. C
6. J

Page 95
1. W
2. N
3. W
4. W
5. W
6. W
7. W
8. N
9. N
10. N
11. W
12. W

Page 96
1. B
2. J
3. C
4. H

Page 97
1. B
2. H
3. A
4. J
5. C
6. G
7. C
8. J
9. Answers will vary. Students might mention that automobiles made it possible for people to live farther away from their workplace since they had a means of transportation to and from work.

Page 98
1. B
2. G
3. A
4. H
5. Answers will vary. Students might mention that we might lose potential sources of medicine if they are cleared, or millions of plants, animals, and insects will lose their natural habitats.

Page 99
Mini-Test 3
1. B
2. G
3. C
4. G
5. D
6. H
7. D
8. F
9. B
10. H

Page 100
1. C
2. H
3. A
4. G

Page 101
1. C
2. F
3. A
4. H
5. A
6. H

Page 102
1. D
2. G
3. C
4. J

Page 103
1. D
2. G
3. A
4. H
5. C
6. H

Page 104
Mini-Test 4
1. C
2. H
3. B
4. H
5. B
6. G
7. C
8. G

Pages 107–109 Final Social Studies Test
1. A
2. H
3. D
4. G
5. B
6. G
7. D
8. G
9. B
10. H
11. B
12. H
13. A

14. G
15. C
16. G
17. B
18. H
19. D
20. G
21. D
22. G
23. C
24. G
25. B
26. J
27. D
28. J
29. A
30. H

Page 113
1. S
2. S
3. N
4. S
5. S
6. S
7. S
8. S
9. S
10. N
11. N
12. S
13. C

Page 114
1. B
2. H
3. D
4. F
5. A

Page 115
1. E
2. O
3. O
4. C
5. E
6. O
7. C
8. E
9. C
10. E
11. O

NOTES

NOTES